COLLECTOR'S COMPASS™

Movie Collectibles

Martingale™
& COMPANY

Credits

President . . . . Nancy J. Martin
CEO . . . . Daniel J. Martin
Publisher . . . . Jane Hamada
Editorial Director . . . . Mary V. Green
Editorial Project Manager . . . . .Tina Cook
Series Editor . . . . Christopher J. Kuppig
Copy Editor . . . . Allison A. Merrill
Design and Production Manager . . . . Stan Green
Series Designer . . . . Bonnie Mather
Production Designer . . . . Jennifer LaRock Shontz
Series Concept . . . . Michael O. Campbell
Studio Photographer . . . . Brent Kane

Collector's Compass™: Movie Collectibles
© 2001 by Martingale & Company

Martingale & Company
20205 144th Avenue NE
Woodinville, WA 98072-8478 USA
www.martingale-pub.com

Printed in Canada
06 05 04 03 02 01   8 7 6 5 4 3 2 1

Cover image ©2001 by Corbis Stock Market/Ford Smith Studio.

Library of Congress Cataloging-in-Publication Data
Movie collectibles.
    p. cm. — (Collector's compass)
  Includes bibliographical references and index.
  ISBN 1-56477-376-0
    1. Motion pictures—Collectibles—Catalogs. I. Series.

PN1995.9.C53 M68 2001
791.43'075—dc21   2001022223

Mission Statement

We are dedicated to providing quality products and service by working
together to inspire creativity and to enrich the lives we touch.

CONTENTS

Foreword   4

Introduction   5

Collecting Movie Memorabilia   7

Essential Background on Movie Memorabilia   19

Before You Start Collecting   29

Photo Gallery   49

Now That You're Ready to Start Collecting   65

Living with Your Collection   89

If and When You Decide to Sell   105

Resources to Further Your Collecting   114

Representative Value Guide   119

Glossary   121

Bibliography and Recommended Reading   122

About the International Society of Appraisers   124

About the Contributors   125

Index   127

FOREWORD

As America's favorite hobby, collecting is exciting, gratifying, and above all, fun—but without the right knowledge, you could be destined for disappointment. Luckily, you've just found the most resourceful and inspiring series of guidebooks available to help you learn more about collecting. The Collector's Compass series approaches collecting in a whole new way, making it easy to learn about your favorite collectible categories—from the basics to the best-kept secrets.

The International Society of Appraisers (ISA) is pleased to be associated with the Collector's Compass series. As the ISA celebrates twenty years of professional education and certification of personal-property appraisers, who currently specialize in more than two hundred areas of expertise, we remain committed to setting the highest standards for our accredited members. The Collector's Compass series of reference books reflects the ISA's dedication to quality and integrity.

Christian Coleman, ISA CAPP, Retired
Executive Director, International Society of Appraisers

INTRODUCTION

Whether it means setting the alarm clock for Saturday morning yard sales, watching *Antiques Roadshow,* or chasing down childhood memories on eBay, collecting has become America's favorite hobby. The joy of finding treasure amid the clutter of a tag sale or a screen full of online offerings is infectious. Who could resist a pastime that combines the fun of shopping, the thrill of the hunt, the lure of a bargain, and the pride of ownership?

Throngs of novice collectors are joining experienced veterans in online bidding and weekend antiquing expeditions. If you count yourself among them, this book is for you.

The editors of the Collector's Compass series realized that today's collectors need more information than what was then obtainable, in an accessible and convenient format. Going beyond available price and identification guides, each Collector's Compass book introduces the history behind a particular collectible, the fascinating aspects that make it special, and exclusive tips on where and how to search for exciting pieces.

Furthermore, the Collector's Compass series is uniquely reliable. Each volume is created by a carefully chosen team of dealers, appraisers, collectors, and other experts. Their collaboration ensures that each title will contain accurate and current information, as well as the secrets they've learned in a lifetime of collecting.

We hope that in the Collector's Compass series we have addressed every area essential to building a collection. Whether you're a newcomer or an experienced collector, we're sure this series will lead you to new treasures. Enjoy the adventure!

*The terrifying motion picture
from the terrifying No. 1 best seller.*

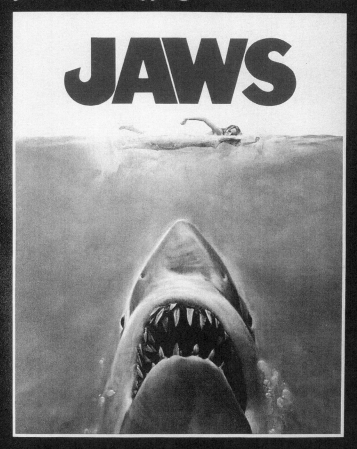

JAWS

**ROY
SCHEIDER** **ROBERT
SHAW** **RICHARD
DREYFUSS**

JAWS

Co-starring LORRAINE GARY · MURRAY HAMILTON · A ZANUCK/BROWN PRODUCTION
Screenplay by PETER BENCHLEY and CARL GOTTLIEB · Based on the novel by PETER BENCHLEY · Music by JOHN WILLIAMS
Directed by STEVEN SPIELBERG · Produced by RICHARD D. ZANUCK and DAVID BROWN · A UNIVERSAL PICTURE ·
TECHNICOLOR® PANAVISION®   **PG** PARENTAL GUIDANCE SUGGESTED
SOME MATERIAL MAY NOT BE
SUITABLE FOR PRE-TEENAGERS   ORIGINAL SOUNDTRACK AVAILABLE ON MCA RECORDS & TAPES
...MAY BE TOO <u>INTENSE</u> FOR YOUNGER CHILDREN

COLLECTING MOVIE MEMORABILIA

The Appeal of Movie Memorabilia

Who doesn't look back and smile thinking of the Saturday afternoons we spent at the movies as kids? The movie theater was a place you could escape to and forget about the trials and tribulations of growing up. Is it any wonder that now, as adults, many collectors seek out movie posters and memorabilia from the films that made indelible early impressions on them? And today, they can actually buy an original poster or lobby card that hung in a theater back when they first saw *Jaws* or *The War of the Worlds,* twenty-five or even fifty years ago.

Movie posters (together with their "paper partners"—lobby cards, photographic stills, press books, and press kits) are the most visible and popular of movie collectibles. But they're by no means the only game in town. There are collectors who don't own a single poster but do own dozens or even hundreds of movie magazines and other items of paper ephemera, books on films and stars, movie character figurals and toys, stars' autographs, sheet music and sound-track albums, licensed tie-in merchandise—including celluloid pin-back buttons, tobacco trading cards, jewelry, limited-edition plates and other ceramics—plus countless "kitschy" souvenir

Opposite: *Jaws,* 1975, Universal, one-sheet. Steven Spielberg's second feature film set a box-office record—broken by *Star Wars* in 1977. *Photo courtesy of Todd Feiertag.*

items relating to films or bearing stars' images. There's even a small, well-heeled group of people who collect the props and costumes used in film production. These folks may be drawn more to specific movie stars—or even tinsel town in general—than to the films of Hollywood's golden age. And if they're captivated by a particular film, such as *The Wizard of Oz* or *Star Wars,* they may collect only items relating to it, such as limited-edition plates, props, costumes, or action figures. Like the movies themselves, the world of movie collectibles has something to satisfy everyone's taste, interest, and budget.

Because this field of collecting is so rich and diverse (not to mention ever-changing, as both classic and current films now are appearing in expanded and enhanced versions on DVD), we've chosen to cover it a bit differently than in other volumes of the Collector's Compass series. The main chapter narratives will discuss the most popular movie collectibles—posters and other paper memorabilia. And in numerous sidebars throughout these chapters, we'll touch on the range of ancillary movie-star and Hollywood collectibles—everything from the *Funny Girl* costumes worn by Barbra Streisand to James Dean commemorative sewing thimbles (yes, they're out there).

Why Posters Rule

Movie posters seem to have an appeal that goes beyond mere nostalgia. Aesthetically, they exert an almost magnetic attraction. No surprise—after all, they were designed to lure patrons into the theater. Especially before movie ads and trailers began to appear on television, studios depended almost exclusively on posters and newspaper advertising (which often used the same images in black-and-white) to build traffic for their newest releases.

The earliest posters, from the 1920s and 1930s, are especially prized for their vibrant visual qualities. Unlike the posters that followed, most of which were printed less expensively on offset presses, early posters were produced using a stone-lithography technique that made the most of their specially commissioned illustrations by Al Hirschfeld, James Montgomery Flagg, Alberto Vargas, Norman Rockwell, and other prominent artists of the day.

Fortunately for the novice, it's possible to begin collecting posters at any level. Two cases in point: A particular style of one-sheet poster for the 1931 release of *Dracula,* of which only two examples are known to exist, might approach $100,000 on the collectors' market. But the readily available *Star Wars: Episode One* poster can be had for as little as $5.

Where to Find Movie Memorabilia

Since items in many categories of movie memorabilia—especially posters—were produced for theater use only, they weren't accessible to the general public in the way that collectible comic books, stamps, and trading cards were. What's more, they weren't manufactured in the huge quantities of these mass-market collectibles, making them more scarce from the outset. But don't despair—our insider tips will point you in the right directions to find the pieces you're looking for.

- **Garage sales, rummage sales, and tag sales.** Don't waste your time shopping here for movie posters or stills. Unless you're lucky enough to stumble upon a seller who worked in a theater or in the motion-picture industry, you'll come away empty-handed. But if you're looking for a *Star Wars* light saber . . .

- **Estate sales and auctions.** These seldom pan out for the poster collector, either. Unless the ad for the sale or auction specifically mentions movie memorabilia, pass on it.

- **Flea markets.** Although it may be a bit of a long shot, occasionally movie posters do surface at these events. And when they do, it's almost a sure bet that they'll go for lots less than they'd command from a specialized dealer or at auction.

- **Specialized dealers.** Specialized movie-memorabilia dealers have access to the latest prices through auction catalogs and price guides, and so are usually fairly knowledgeable about what their merchandise is worth. Expect to pay top dollar or close to it when you shop here. But specialized dealers are more likely to have exactly what you're looking for, so the time they save you in searching other venues without results could be considerable.

- **Specialized collectibles shows.** Collectibles shows geared specifically to movie memorabilia are excellent sources for the collector. The biggest shows are held in California and New York, but others are held all across the country. Full-time dealers sell here, of course, but so do other collectors, giving you the opportunity to negotiate prices on the things you're interested in.
- **Trade papers**. Publications devoted to movie posters and memorabilia, such as *Movie Collector's World, Big Reel, Films of the Golden Age,* and *Classic Images,* can be excellent sources.
- **Online auctions and live auctions.** Internet auction sites, such as eBay, and auction houses, such as Sotheby's and Christie's, are where you'll come across the better and scarcer memorabilia that you just won't find anywhere else. Although you can certainly snag bargains at auction, you're more likely to pay top dollar.

How to Organize Your Collection

For a collectible category as freewheeling and fun as movie memorabilia, it may seem a bit pedantic to talk about "organizing" a collection. But that's precisely what collectors do—even if subconsciously—in deciding what to buy. Here are some of the most popular themes.

- **By genre.** Whether it's horror, science fiction, Western, or film noir, genre seems to be the most popular way to assemble a collection. Science fiction and horror are probably the two most popular genres, and their memorabilia tends to be the most flamboyant visually.
- **By film.** It may be *The Wizard of Oz, Star Wars,* or *Casablanca;* if it's a great movie, there is an enthusiastic coterie of collectors obsessed with it. They want to own an example of everything they can find relating to their particular film.
- **By star.** For every movie star, dead or alive, there's someone collecting his or her images, in whatever form—from movie-star fanzines to studio portraits.
- **By artist.** Posters by artists such as Saul Bass, Alberto Vargas, Al Hirschfeld, and others have become sought-after collectibles.

- **By studio.** Some collectors focus on posters from a specific movie studio, such as MGM, Warner Bros., Paramount, or Universal.
- **By printer.** Others collect posters printed by a particular lithographic company, such as Morgan Litho, H. C. Minor Litho, Joseph H. Tooker, or Ritchey Litho.

The Omnivorous Collector

Can't decide on a particular film category? Then you might take a cue from a well-known collector who aims to possess something from *every movie ever made*. Try to imagine the tens of thousands of films produced over the past hundred years and you'll get a sense of what a monumental task this has been. Not surprisingly, this collector has had to commandeer an empty bank building just to store it all!

Values and Trends

As a new or aspiring collector of movie memorabilia, you no doubt have lots of questions about the field, and perhaps specifically about the economics of collecting such things as posters, press books, and stills. Here, courtesy of some longtime and savvy collectors, are definitive answers.

Is this a good time to start collecting movie posters?

Even though people have been collecting movie posters for many years, the field is still fairly young. There's tremendous potential for growth. For many years, collectors formed a small, close-knit group of people who all knew each other by name and often by sight, from dealings over the phone, through the mail, and from shows and auctions. Today, as the mass media and especially the Internet have educated people about the collectibility and value of movie posters, all that has changed. New collectors are entering the marketplace every day.

What's the investment potential of collecting movie posters?

It's pretty darn good. In the past three years alone, prices for most posters have at least held constant, and for many they have more than doubled. In the past five years, some have appreciated 200 to 300 percent.

From Russia with Love, 1964, United Artists, still. Apparently considered too racy, Daniela Bianchi's exposed thigh was blacked out by the studio! *Photo courtesy of Michael B. King.*

Bond . . . James Bond

In 1965, Sean Connery was the No. 1 box-office draw in the world, largely because of his cool and sexy character in the spy-thriller film series based on Ian Fleming's novels. James Bond, whether played by Connery or any of the other actors who followed him in the role, always bested the bizarre villain, always got the heroine with the suggestive name, and had a license to kill. In all Bond flicks, the audience was treated to cleverly deadly special effects, and these form the basis for the most popular Bond movie collectibles. Just owning one makes you cool.

At the more affordable end of the range, a deck of plastic-coated *Tomorrow Never Dies* promotional playing cards may be had for $10. An unlicensed 1960s pistol ring in the original package sells for $10 to $30. And a copy of a 1964 *James Bond 007* magazine costs $20 to $60. For the more advanced collector, the James Bond Secret Agent Presentation Set, by Lone Star—including repeating cap pistol, silencer, holster, secret-agent badge, and ID card—has sold at auction for nearly $650. Both of two versions of Corgi's die-cast Aston Martin DB5 topped out at $500 to $600. There's a Gilbert 12½" James Bond 007 action figure, made in 1965, that went for $1,200. The attaché case by Multiple Products—complete with codebook, rifle, bullets, "code-o-matic," billfold and money, business cards, rubber knife, and instructions—reached $1,367 at the all-Bond auction held by Christie's South Kensington in February 2001. But the big kahuna of that auction (which undoubtedly raised the value bar overall for Bond collectibles) was one of two 1965 Aston Martin DB5 sports cars used in the chase scene in *GoldenEye*. The silver beauty with black interior was hammered down, including buyer's premium, for more than $229,000!

Novice collectors may find it easier and more affordable to start with items from the later Bond movies. Online auction sites such as eBay have recently featured an array of them, from the *GoldenEye* board game at $30 to a set of nine metal Heineken beer James Bond coasters at $18.50. There are also trading cards, action figures, and DVDs of the Bond movies.

Beware items that have no real association with the films other than that Bond "had one like it." An example: the Omega Seamaster watch, which has been touted in Omega ads as "James Bond's favorite."

To see items, make contact with other collectors, and learn about the annual Bond collectors' weekend, visit the James Bond for Sale or Trade Web site. Nick Bennett's Collection of 007 Memorabilia Web site features an extensive collection (with emphasis on Pierce Brosnan), some of which is for sale.

To learn more:
- *O'Brien's Collecting Toys,* Elizabeth Stephan, editor
- *A Collector's Guide to Movie Star Memorabilia,* Brian Mills
- *Hake's Price Guide to Character Toy Premiums,* Ted Hake
- James Bond for Sale or Trade Web site:
  www.members.tripod.com/~msherm/index.html
- Nick Bennett's Collection of 007 Memorabilia Web site:
  www.lasercc.demon.co.uk/bond.htm

The highest price ever paid for a poster of any kind was paid at an auction at Sotheby's in New York on March 1, 1997. A one-sheet for *The Mummy* from 1932, with Boris Karloff and Zita Johann, more than doubled the previous record of $198,000 set in October 1993 for a one-sheet from *Frankenstein* (1931). One of only two known copies, *The Mummy* poster sold for a record-breaking $453,500.

If movie posters are so valuable, aren't prices likely to be inflated?

It's true—horror and science-fiction posters are extremely popular and do bring high prices. But over time they've consistently risen in value. For new collectors, the best advice is to shop around. If you make a habit of checking with several dealers, you'll discover that there's a wide range of prices—and you'll probably save yourself some money on your eventual purchases.

Are there still opportunities to "Buy low and sell high" with movie posters?

Of course, although it's getting harder all the time. But even today, at live auctions and in Internet auctions, there are many pieces that fall through the cracks. Our best advice for snapping up these bargains is to get a good general education on what collectible posters are worth.

What about posters for American-produced films in international release?

American poster collectors by and large shun the posters created by distributors for American-produced films in their international releases. However, the translations of film titles and copy are sometimes wryly amusing, and it's not uncommon for the graphics used by international-market distributors to have superior quality and impact. On the other hand, posters for non-U.S. films in U.S. distribution are desired and actively collected.

What's the "profile" of someone who collects movie memorabilia?

Even though there are now many more women who collect movie posters than there were several years ago, the majority of collectors are men, in their twenties to fifties.

Are there any celebrities who collect movie posters?

Yes, indeed—lots of them. Director Martin Scorsese collects posters and hangs them in his offices on Park Avenue in New York. Leonardo Di Caprio is beginning to collect them, and seems to like early horror and *Star Wars* posters. Kirk Hammett, lead guitarist for Metallica, also collects classic horror and science-fiction material. Michael Jackson has been collecting for many years, favoring Three Stooges posters and posters of child actors including Shirley Temple and Freddie Bartholomew. Nicholas Cage has recently started acquiring some rare and desirable horror posters. Producer-director-writer-actor Ron Howard collects fine examples of classic movie posters.

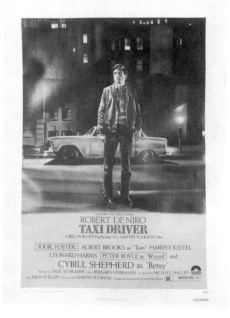

Star Wars, 1978, Twentieth Century Fox, one-sheet, Style D with sound-track promotion. This poster for the first *Star Wars* movie sold for $1,265 in 1999, but a poster for *Star Wars Episode One* can be had for as little as $5. *Photo courtesy of Skinner, Inc.*

Taxi Driver, 1976, Columbia, one-sheet. Collectors love this powerful film with a seemingly alienating hero. *Photo courtesy of Chisholm-Larsson Gallery.*

15

Hush … Hush, Sweet Charlotte, 1964, Twentieth Century Fox, one-sheet. A memorable cast in a macabre story. *Photo courtesy of Chisholm-Larsson Gallery.*

Kitsch

The Merriam-Webster's Collegiate Dictionary defines kitsch as "something that appeals to popular or lowbrow taste and is often of poor quality." In terms of collectible kitsch, we talk about "novelty items," and they're some of the most popular film collectibles on the market. Their appeal derives from their tastelessness: they're so bad, they're cool. And they're usually cheap.

Take these examples: The James Dean thimble, manufactured in 1985 by an unknown American company, may seem an unlikely place to find the image of a cult movie hero. But on second thought, it may not be so surprising: the item would appeal both to collectors of commemorative thimbles and to James Dean aficionados. The thimble currently sells for $10 to $15. It is eclipsed in tastelessness by the James Dean musical snow globe, featuring a full-length image of Dean inside the globe, which is mounted on a base showing a Porsche Spyder (the car in which he was killed) and a cowboy hat. The music box plays the Beatles' "Yesterday." It recently sold for $53 on eBay.

No movie star has been "kitsched" more than Marilyn Monroe. Her image, both clothed and unclothed, has appeared on everything from drinking glasses and calendars to notepads and plates. The famous nude calendar pose on a base-metal money clip will set a collector back about $15; a silver-plated spoon with her portrait will cost only $3.

Finding kitsch movie items should be no problem at all: they're everywhere. Look in flea markets and tourist-area gift shops—antiques dealers and the better auction houses usually won't carry them. And, of course, there are the Internet auction sites such as eBay, where you'll see them listed by the hundreds. Just type in the name of a favorite star to bring up pages of novelty items.

There aren't any pitfalls in buying this stuff. It's all so cheaply made that no one would produce copies, so there are no fakes to worry about. And it's ubiquitous, so it pays to do some comparison shopping to get the lowest price.

To learn more:
- *The James Dean Collector's Guide,* David Loehr and Joe Bills
- *A Collector's Guide to Movie Star Memorabilia,* Brian Mills
- *Starstruck: The Wonderful World of Movie Memorabilia,* Robert Heide and John Gilman

Charlie Chaplin His Signature

IN HIS THIRD MILLION DOLLAR COMEDY

"SUNNYSIDE"

A "First National" Attraction

ESSENTIAL BACKGROUND ON MOVIE MEMORABILIA

The First Movie Posters

No sooner had motion pictures debuted in the mid-1890s, with the films of the Lumière brothers in France and Thomas Edison in the United States, than the field of collectible movie memorabilia was born. Several of the very first posters created to introduce this new medium to the public depicted audience members held spellbound as they watch ghostly images on the huge screen before them, with beams of light coming from a projector behind. It's the same magical aura that attracts us to stadium theaters today—and to collectible movie memorabilia.

It wasn't until about 1910, when movie stars such as Mary Pickford and Charlie Chaplin were being introduced to the American moviegoing public, that film studios began to employ photographers to promote their new films and players. By the '20s and '30s, the Hollywood publicity machine included scores of photographers, who churned out a blizzard of images—portraits of stars, scene stills, and production shots—which were sent to fan magazines and newspapers and were turned into posters, lobby displays, "coming attractions" glass lantern slides, banners, and

Sunnyside, 1919, First National, one-sheet. In 1918, when Charlie Chaplin, an international celebrity after his fifth year in movies, signed a contract with First National Pictures, he was paid more than one million dollars for eight two-reel films. This poster's portraits epitomize the art of hand-crayoned stone lithography. *Photo courtesy of Michael B. King.*

more. Little did they know at the time that they were creating some of the most prized collectibles of the century.

When a film's theatrical run was over, posters were supposed to be returned to the studios' "exchanges" (in exchange for a set to publicize the next feature), but much of this material was routinely discarded. Years later, World War II paper drives consumed many of the movie posters that had survived, making the pre-1940 examples that remain today even rarer. Fortunately, some theater managers followed the rules and returned posters, lobby cards, stills, and other materials to exchanges for reuse by second-run houses. Others stockpiled them in storage rooms. On occasion, materials that had been thrown out were rescued by projectionists, ushers, or studio or theater employees before the trash collector arrived.

The Golden Age of Movie Posters

The golden age of movie posters, and photo stills as well, coincides with the rise and fall of the great Hollywood studios in the 1920s through the 1950s. With the advent of television, the studios shifted away from print to this novel medium to sell their stars and films. Even though posters and photographs of the stars are still produced today, aficionados consider them vastly inferior to the best examples from Hollywood's golden age.

Not surprisingly, among the items that have become the most highly prized are early posters, which range in size from the 11" x 14" lobby cards (usually issued in sets of eight) to the billboard-size twenty-four-sheets that measure 9' x 20'. Unlike baseball cards and comic books, movie posters were never meant to be sold to the public. Some even carry a printed warning at the bottom: "This advertising material is leased and not sold. It is the property of [the studio] and upon completion of the exhibition for which it has been leased by the exhibitor, it should be returned to the [studio] exchange." Studio exchanges, located in major markets, distributed posters, prints, and other publicity materials to theater owners. After 1941, when the National Screen Service (NSS) was contracted by the industry to act as the studios' one-stop clearinghouse for posters and trailers, the legend stipulated that materials should be returned to the NSS. Although some nervous collectors have been known to trim stills of this legend, or black it out with a marking pen, this is an unnecessary precaution. The warning was intended to remind theater owners that the material wasn't their property to sell at the time. Today, most dealers simply acknowledge that the sale of these items is for personal use only and that all other rights are held by the copyright owners.

Movie Paper Formats

- Midget window cards (vertical): 8" x 14" (blank at top for theater imprint)
- Mini window cards (vertical): 10" x 18" (blank at top for theater imprint)
- Lobby cards (horizontal): 11" x 14"
- Jumbo lobby cards (horizontal or vertical): 14" x 17"
- Window cards (vertical): 14" x 22" (blank at top for theater imprint)
- Jumbo window cards (vertical): 22" x 28" (blank at top for theater imprint)
- Inserts (vertical): 14" x 36"
- Displays or half-sheets (horizontal): 22" x 28"
- One-sheets (vertical): 27" x 41"
- Three-sheets (three individual sheets horizontal, complete image vertical; later, two individual sheets horizontal, complete image vertical): 41" x 81"
- 30" x 40" (vertical)
- 40" x 60" (vertical)
- Six-sheets (four sections, complete image square): 81" x 81"
- Twenty-four-sheets (horizontal): 9' x 20'

Materials and Manufacture

The most prized and collectible movie posters—those produced from the 1920s through the 1950s—have a unique look and feel. First, the paper on which most were printed is a delicate newsprint. Second, early posters were printed with a stone-lithography process, which made the most of the vibrant artistry of their graphics and illustrations. But by the 1930s the less costly color photo-offset process was used more frequently, and the overall effect just can't compare with the classic lithographed examples. Posters printed by color offset are generally on heavier, gloss-coated paper, so if you

Metropolis, 1926, UFA/Paramount, lobby card. This lobby card for one of the first and most haunting science-fiction films fetched $10,925 in 1999. *Photo courtesy of Skinner, Inc.*

ever come across a poster for the 1932 film *The Mummy* and it's on glossy paper, you can be sure it's a reproduction, not an original!

Another tip-off that a particular poster may not be a rare original-issue is its size. Whereas reproductions of older posters usually are slightly smaller (or larger) than the originals, the real things were consistently printed in standard sizes (see "Movie Paper Formats" on page 21).

Posters in the one-sheet size (27" x 41", oriented vertically) are by far the most common. From the 1920s through the 1950s, virtually all one-sheets were folded flat after printing to facilitate storage and shipping to theaters. So, if you ever come across a rolled (i.e., never been folded) one-sheet from a vintage film, it's probably a reproduction.

How Movie Posters Became Collectible

The Early Appeal of Movie Posters

The earliest collectors of movie posters and memorabilia were mostly theater owners, projectionists, ushers, distributors, and publicists. As industry insiders, they already had a strong feeling for the material. Just as important, they knew where posters, stills, and other items could be found. And with each passing decade, they became more and more nostalgic for the films that had gone before.

Books

Books about films and film stars are a wonderful category for beginning collectors because they're so affordable. Most sell for under $20, and many volumes can be had for much less.

Celebrity biographies and autobiographies almost always can be purchased cheaply, possibly because the revelations in them, once they're "out of the bag," no longer have much allure. Some notable exceptions are books by or about major stars who led colorful lives. A 1946 illustrated biography of Orson Welles recently sold for more than $100. *Peekaboo,* an unauthorized biography of Veronica Lake, is valued at approximately $60.

Books about the making of films are similarly low-priced, unless they treat major hits and contain behind-the-scenes photos or scripts. *Making Ghostbusters,* by Dan Ackroyd, which includes both, sells for $50 and up. *Star Wars Chronicles,* by D. Fine, which includes production stills, outtakes, and other material from the Lucasfilm archives, is valued at around $100.

As with all paper collectibles, condition is especially important in this category, with rarity and popularity of the film or star close behind. Used-book stores, flea markets, and charity book sales are great places to look for books on films and star biographies. eBay has a category for "Books Movies Music>Memorabilia." Within that category are the subcategories "celebrity," "movies," and "movie: current." Any of these categories may be searched, using the keywords "book," "biography," or "autobiography." Or, search on a star's name, the title of a film, or even the director's name. Concentrate on what appeals to you, and try to buy it in excellent condition.

To learn more:

- www.CollectingChannel.com—type "movies" into the box "Find Your Passion"
- *A Collector's Guide to Movie Star Memorabilia,* Brian Mills
- *Huxford's Old Book Value Guide,* Bob Huxford and Sharon Huxford

The Films of Myrna Loy by Lawrence J. Quirk, published in 1980, out of print. This catalog of Loy's films includes entertaining film descriptions and gorgeous black-and-white stills. The series *The Films of ...* is a must for any collector's library.

Movie Memorabilia Comes into Its Own

In the spring of 1990, the "Legends of Film and Rock" auction was held by Camden House in Los Angeles, when 647 items, including posters and lobby cards, were sold for $750,000. With major auction houses Christie's and Sotheby's following suit, a genuine boom was inaugurated in the poster market. *Entertainment Weekly* stated, in a story by Barbara Ettore in its issue dated January 11, 1991, "Many movie posters had soared in value by 500 percent or more in the '80s." Also in 1990, with the appearance of the book *Poster Price Almanac,* the field finally achieved an organization and legitimacy that had been lacking. As editor John Kisch states in his introduction to the annual review, "Nowhere else can dealers and collectors find, in one place, such a complete and constructive record of the past year's offerings and sales." This volume has become indispensable to anyone involved in the field.

Movie Memorabilia for the Masses

Now, with more than 50 percent of American homes plugged in to the Internet, the entire world has become one immense "dealers' room," available at any time of night or day with the click of a mouse. Using online resources, dealers and collectors are buying and selling material on auction sites such as eBay, as well as creating their own Web pages. More people are involved in collecting movie memorabilia than ever before. It's all out there: a poster from Brad Pitt's *Fight Club* (1999), a lobby card from Garbo's *Romance* (1930), a glass slide from Fritz Lang's *Metropolis* (1926), a suit that Mickey Rourke wore in *9½ Weeks* (1986).

In addition, today there are shows and conventions dedicated to the trading and selling of posters and other movie memorabilia. Cinefest in Syracuse, New York, and Cinevent in Columbus, Ohio, are two regularly scheduled shows that are musts for both novice and veteran collectors. The Hollywood Collectors & Celebrities Show, held regularly in North Hollywood, San Francisco, and Chicago, is a huge event noted for appearances by Hollywood stars. It's at events like these that one meets dealers and fellow collectors and gets to see and buy rare original material.

Posters are the darling of the movie-collectible field at the moment, no doubt because of their colorful and strikingly printed graphic designs. They don't pretend to be fine art, but they have an impact, a sense of fun, and a vitality that's uniquely American. At their best—and worst—they tell a fascinating story about our values and fantasies as few of the graphic arts can.

Planet of the Apes, 1968, Twentieth Century Fox, one-sheet. Great fun, if not exactly great moviemaking. *Photo courtesy of Chisholm-Larsson Gallery.*

Figurals, Dolls, and Toys

When movie producers first began to market figurals and other toys as a way of promoting their films, they probably didn't suspect that movie character items would become the world's most popular toy collectible. Today, these toys aren't just for kids, and those at the upper end of the price spectrum are definitely not for play. At the more affordable end are board games associated with the movies, which range in price from $5 for a movie-trivia game to $100 for a 1949 Drive-In Theatre Movie Game with cowboy cover. Figures and dolls range from a 1998 nine-inch talking Austin Powers doll at $6 to a 1940 Ideal Judy Garland doll in her *Strike Up the Band* costume for $1,000. Puzzles depicting posters from hit movies cost about $5. Plastic models and figures range from a *Toy Story* Mr. Potato Head at $8 to a *Robocop* ED-209 at $150.

Austin Powers action figure from McFarlane Toys. *Photo courtesy of McFarlane Toys.*

There's a whole class of toys that are desirable just because they're odd. A horror-movie makeup kit from Pressman will run $79, and that's for makeup that's forty years old!

And then there are the Westerns. Cowboy material is wildly popular, with cap guns topping the list at an average of $400 a set if they're still in their holsters. Specific cowboys also mean big bucks: a Roy Rogers cardboard-and-plastic guitar in the original box sells for $200.

No discussion of movie figurals, dolls, and toys would be complete without a mention of Shirley Temple, known to the public as America's Sweetheart and to the studios as Our Little Cash Cow. Thousands of Shirley Temple items were produced, and some, like the 1939 doll in costume from the movie *Blue Bird,* which sells for $4,500 and up, are very hot collectibles indeed.

You'll find these items everywhere, from the Internet to auctions to specialized doll-and-toy shows. On eBay, it's best to search in the toy category instead of the movie category.

As with any toy, having the box in good condition can double or even triple the value of the item. The Roy Rogers guitar mentioned above sells for $200 with the box but only $75 without it.

Beware unlicensed copies, some of which are very cheaply produced. They lack detail, and can actually be quite ugly. However, some collectors like to include them for that very reason. It's also important to be sure that toys are in working order; examine them carefully for repairs. A nonworking toy, unless it's extremely rare, is virtually worthless, and a repaired toy is worth far less than one in original condition. Get a written receipt with a complete description from the dealer.

To learn more:
- eBay "Toys" category
- *Hake's Price Guide to Character Toy Premiums,* Ted Hake
- *Hake's Guide to Cowboy Character Collectibles,* Ted Hake
- *Shirley Temple Dolls and Fashions,* Edward R. Pardella
- *The Judy Garland Collector's Guide,* Edward R. Pardella
- *The James Dean Collector's Guide,* David Loehr and Joe Bills

They sold their souls for...

"THE TREASURE OF THE SIERRA MADRE"

STARRING

HUMPHREY BOGART

WARNER BROS.
hit a new high in high adventure...
bringing another great best-seller
to the screen!

WALTER HUSTON · TIM HOLT · BRUCE BENNETT

DIRECTED BY
JOHN HUSTON · HENRY BLANKE
PRODUCED BY

BEFORE YOU START COLLECTING

What You Need to Know about the Marketplace

As you're about to see, there's no single marketplace for movie posters and memorabilia. Rather, the collective marketplace consists of everything from hole-in-the-wall poster dealers to high-end auctions at well-known houses such as Christie's and Sotheby's. Here are tips on some of the most important.

Garage Sales, Yard Sales, and Tag Sales

If you find any posters at garage sales, yard sales, or tag sales, they're likely to be newer reproductions or video-release posters, neither of which is of much interest to serious collectors. However, if you're willing to spend a few dollars to have a favorite image for decorative use, or as a "placeholder" until you find an original, you may be satisfied with what you're likely to find in this sector.

Estate Sales and Estate Auctions

You'll probably fare better at estate sales and estate auctions than at garage and tag sales. Ads sometimes contain detailed listings of sale items; it pays to scrutinize them for posters or anything related to movies.

Opposite: *The Treasure of the Sierra Madre,* 1948, Warner Bros., one-sheet. Surprisingly, Humphrey Bogart's standout performance as a paranoid gold prospector wasn't even nominated for an Academy Award. *Photo courtesy of Chisholm-Larsson Gallery.*

The Golden Rules of Collecting

1. Buy Quality, Not Quantity

If you collect John Wayne Western posters, for example, try collecting a few from the original 1930s and 1940s releases, for which he's most famous, instead of less desirable posters from rereleases.

2. Invest in Reference Books and Magazines

Subscribe to collectors' publications such as *Movie Collector's World* and *Big Reel*. And the *Poster Price Almanac* by John Kisch is a must.

3. Collect What You Like

Collect something because you *like* it, not because you think it's going to be worth a lot of money someday.

4. Be Active

The more you stay in touch with other collectors and dealers, the more knowledgeable you'll become, and the more quickly you'll find the items you're seeking.

5. Be Patient

For most posters from the 1950s to the present, try shopping around rather than buying the first example you see. You'll probably find another in the same (or better) condition, possibly for less money.

6. Be Fair

Be fair and honest with other collectors and dealers. Poster-collecting circles are small, and a good reputation is one of your greatest assets.

7. Add to the History

Keep good records of the posters you buy. Remember: You're a link in the story each piece has to tell.

8. Nurture Your Personal Vision

Think for yourself. Don't collect a certain star or genre just because people say that's what's hot right now.

9. Be a Good Steward

You own something only until it passes into the hands of the next caring collector, so you should take proper care of it and any accompanying materials that document its history.

Flea Markets and Bazaars

With hundreds of people—full-time dealers as well as amateurs—selling all kinds of merchandise, your chances of finding movie posters and memorabilia here are marginally better than at garage sales and estate sales. While you may find a variety of movie and star-related material in this sector, be wary of mediocre-condition pieces bearing high price tags.

Consignment Shops

Although it's certainly possible to find movie posters and memorabilia at consignment shops, it doesn't happen often.

The Internet

Movie posters and memorabilia abound on the Internet. In fact, it's just about the best place to find them. eBay alone lists more than 60,000 items of movie memorabilia at any one time. You'll find posters offered by dealers, individual collectors, and everyday people who just happened to come across them. Especially when the seller isn't fully aware of the value of what he or she has, it's possible to get some great deals here.

Although they're not as likely to offer bargains, the Web sites of specialist poster dealers are another great Internet resource. Unlike auction sites, dealer sites usually offer merchandise at fixed prices.

Antiques-and-Collectibles Malls

If you should happen to find a movie poster at an antiques-and-collectibles mall, be careful. Many dealers at these venues aren't especially knowledgeable about movie posters and may unknowingly be offering a reproduction. Worse still, the dealer may be

---

It Should Happen to You

One poster collector we know will never forget the estate sale he dropped in to in 1987. The late owner of the house happened to have been a projectionist for a theater in a small town, and he had kept posters and lobby cards dating back to the 1930s. "Some of the best things I ever acquired came from that estate," he told us. "There was even a mint *Frankenstein* lobby-card set that I was able to purchase for a very reasonable price at the time."

asking a lot of money for it just because he or she has heard that movie posters are hot collectibles.

Specialty Shops

In the late '70s, there was only a handful of specialized dealers who made their living selling movie posters. Today, there are hundreds. Many of them advertise in collectors' publications, such as *Movie Collector's World* and *Big Reel,* and in the bible of poster prices, *Poster Price Almanac,* by John Kisch. If you're looking for a particular poster, contact several dealers to compare the price and condition of the examples they're selling.

Antiques-and-Collectibles Shows

Specialized movie-memorabilia shows are infinitely better than general antiques shows for finding exactly what you want. They're almost like going directly to the source!

A notch down in terms of targeting are toy shows and paper-ephemera shows. You may find a few poster dealers at the latter, but if your collecting interests range across the other subjects we've mentioned, you may well find rich and more varied offerings.

If the show takes place at a hotel, as many do, consider showing up the night before. That's when many dealers will already be set up in their rooms—buying, selling, and trading among themselves (called "room hopping"). You may get the opportunity to acquire things before the general public even gets to see them.

Dealer Fixed-Price Catalogs and Auctions

You'll find a variety of dealer fixed-price catalogs and auctions advertised in collectors' publications such as *Movie Collector's World* and *Big Reel.* Dealers who sell by catalog and mail auction usually charge for subscriptions but may offer a sample catalog free. Most auction-catalog subscriptions entitle you to receive a sheet showing prices realized, which can be useful in building your knowledge of current values.

Dealing with Dealers

Dealers are such an important source—for valuable information as well as for memorabilia—that it pays to know the ins and outs of working with them.

James Cagney portrait still from *Angels with Dirty Faces,* 1938, Warner Bros. Cagney delivers a gripping performance in this melodrama about a doomed hoodlum and the tough priest who was his childhood friend. *Photo courtesy of Michael B. King.*

Gold Is Where You Find It

Before you decide to pass entirely on general shows, consider the experience of this collector: "I remember going years ago to a large general paper show in Hartford, Connecticut, and stumbling across a *King Kong* title card [from a set of lobby cards]. The dealer happened to specialize in sports material and wasn't sure if it was from the original release, so he didn't know how to price it. He was asking $150 for it, and I scooped it up. I knew it definitely was from the original release and was worth much more. At that time, its value was at least $1,500 to $2,000. Today, it's worth at least four or five times that."

Can I rely on dealers to know everything there is to know about what they're selling and what it's worth?

No dealer can be expected to know everything about everything. In fact, it's good that they don't—the occasions when you happen to know more about an item than the dealer who's selling it are when you'll snag real bargains. Dealer knowledge varies widely. Savvy collectors ask dealers questions—lots of them. When you do that, you'll soon get a sense of whether the dealer knows what he or she is talking about.

Are most dealers honest?

Fortunately, yes. Dealers who habitually lie to their customers don't stay in business long. But that doesn't let you off the hook: you should still do your homework and ask lots of questions. Dealers aren't out to cheat people, but they aren't always as careful as they might be, either. Never enter into any major purchase ($500 or more) without some sort of written guarantee of authenticity. Any dealer who's unwilling to accommodate you on this doesn't deserve your business.

How can dealers help me build my collection?

Probably in more ways than you can imagine. First, most dealers love to talk about their merchandise and, in so doing, will give you invaluable insights and information. Second, by building a long-term relationship with a dealer you like—by being an active collector who makes regular purchases from that dealer—you'll earn

---

COLLECTOR'S COMPASS

Want-List Wonders

An up-to-date want list in the hands of a dealer who knows you is one of your best hopes of finding the pieces you truly want. Leaving a want list in no way obligates you to buy a particular item, but it does show the dealer that you're serious.

To make the most of your dealer network, you should be willing to pay at or near current market price for the items on your want list. This doesn't necessarily mean top dollar, but you'll find that dealers seldom call collectors who are looking only for "wholesale-price steals."

a spot on the dealer's A-list. You'll be among the first to be called when truly special items appear on the market.

Are dealers' prices ever negotiable?

Certainly. Never be afraid to bargain—it's part of the fun of collecting. In fact, most dealers factor a certain amount of "wiggle room" into their asking price—anywhere from 10 to 20 percent.

Just be sure to keep your negotiations positive. Refrain from pointing out flaws or otherwise insulting the merchandise. If a piece seems expensive, ask the dealer how he arrived at the price. Or you might say something like "Would you be open to an offer on this piece?" or "Is there any room on the price?" If you'll be paying cash, now's the time to mention it. This sometimes works to your advantage when you're negotiating.

Take your time, but if you and the dealer reach common ground in your price negotiations, be prepared to buy. To a dealer, there are few things worse than customers who negotiate as a game and really have no intention of buying.

"I'll Take It!"

A word to the wise: On those supremely memorable occasions when you happen across a sought-after item that's ridiculously underpriced, simply say "I'll take it!"

Don't discuss. Don't negotiate. Just buy it and walk away. The dealer almost certainly will eventually realize his mistake. And although it's fair to buy a bargain, don't add insult to injury by asking for an additional discount.

Is it a good idea to leave a "standing bid" with a dealer for a particular piece?

A standing bid—the highest price you're willing to pay for a piece—actually could end up working against you. A dealer might use your open-ended offer to "shop the piece around," or try to tease out interest at a higher price. Your offer will be more compelling when you say, "I'll buy this piece right now for this price." Of course, that doesn't mean you wouldn't buy it later for the same price, but such a statement might prompt the dealer to act.

The Producers,
1967, Embassy,
insert. One of the
rare comedies that
fans say get funnier
with each viewing.
*Photo courtesy of
Skinner, Inc.*

Should I request a receipt for every purchase?

Yes, definitely. The receipt should include the dealer's name and address, your name, and a description of the piece you've bought (including its approximate age and condition). The exceptions: garage sales and flea markets, where some vendors may not give receipts; at these venues, simply record the details of your purchase in a notebook.

What if I'm not satisfied with my purchase?

It's your responsibility to safeguard your satisfaction. There are a number of things you can and should do before committing to a purchase. First, you should always ask a dealer about his return policy before buying. Some will refund your money if the item is returned in the same condition as when it was sold; others won't (after all, you've taken the item off the market by purchasing it, and have thus deprived the dealer of the opportunity to sell it to someone else). If you have an ongoing relationship with the seller, he'll likely be interested in maintaining your satisfaction. But always ask before buying, and make sure you have a firm understanding.

Second, regardless of who it is you're buying from, getting a receipt that describes the item in detail is your most important line of defense in the event that it turns out to be something other than what it was represented to be. Whenever you buy a high-ticket item, you should ask for a written guarantee of authenticity as additional protection.

If you're dissatisfied with your purchase because of condition, that's another matter. Inspect the piece carefully before you agree to buy it, and ask the seller specific questions about its condition, the originality of all pieces, and any history of repair or restoration. Knowing about flaws and defects is up to you; an upstanding dealer should offer full disclosure, but in practice the burden is on the buyer to pose questions. If you discover that the seller has misrepresented the piece, use your detailed receipt and guarantee of authenticity assertively to get a refund. There's no guarantee that you'll never get burned, but most dealers would rather take an item back than risk acquiring a reputation for unscrupulous practice.

Participating in Auctions

What are the pros and cons of buying in an online auction?

Online auctions have provided greater access to collectibles than has ever existed before. They've leveled the playing field, giving people in all areas of the country—and around the world—equal opportunity to sell and bid on items.

However, online auctions have introduced an unprecedented number of essentially sight-unseen transactions. No matter how much care and detail the seller puts into his description or how clear his digital photos are, it's not the same as examining the item in the flesh. While the vast majority of online transactions turn out well for both buyer and seller, if you're unsure about bidding—especially on a high-ticket item—don't hesitate to inquire about the item's condition and authenticity or request additional photos. And be sure to ask for a guarantee that you'll be able to return the piece for a full refund if it's not in the condition advertised.

Where can I find online auctions?

By visiting any search engine and entering "online auctions" as your search term, you'll generate a long list of auction sites on the Internet. eBay, at www.ebay.com, is the most popular one.

How do I register for an online auction?

On eBay, one of the first headings you'll see on the home page is for a "New User" section. This explains the details of bidding and selling, both of which require you to register. To register, you must have an e-mail address. You then access the registration page and enter personal information such as your name, address, and e-mail address. You'll find the eBay registration page at: http://pages.ebay.com/services/registration/register.html.

In order to sell items, you'll have to place a credit-card number on file. There's usually a small fee charged for placing an item on auction and then a commission charged when the item sells. These charges are made directly to your credit-card account and are summarized on monthly statements you'll receive from the auction site.

Props, Costumes, Scripts, Scenery, and Frames

Demand for the actual articles used in films, such as props, costumes, scripts, and scenery, has spawned a huge facsimile industry. Scores of special-effects studios, licensed manufacturers, and amateur entrepreneurs aggressively market copies of items from blockbuster hits. This is especially true of science-fiction and fantasy movies. These replicas sell like hotcakes, at least in part because the real thing has become too pricey for the average collector. The stunning period gown worn by Barbra Streisand while she sang "People" in *Funny Girl* recently sold for $5,200, but a pair of handmade boots like those worn by Bobba Fett of *Star Wars* sells for about $200.

A word about frames: Virtually all of the 16 mm and 35 mm mounted single frames found on the market are made from prints of films which have been cut up for sale frame by frame. There's some debate about their true collectibility.

Auctions, both live and on the Internet, are undoubtedly the place to buy authentic film-used items as well as facsimiles. Disney has established an exclusive auction site on eBay. Planet Hollywood, which maintains a warehouse full of props and costumes in Hollywood, runs auctions from eBay as well, some to benefit charities. And both Christie's and Sotheby's

How do I search out the items I'm interested in?

The eBay home page features a "Categories" list with a heading "Books/Movies/Music." Clicking on that link will take you to the page that offers "Memorabilia" as a selection, with sub-selections for "Movie" and "Movie: Current." By clicking on the "Movie" link, you'll arrive at a detailed list of posters (by type and period), press books, stills, props, costumes, and several other sub-categories. Or, try searching on keywords like "lobby card" or "movie poster." If you're looking for material related to a particular film, try the film's title. You might also search stars' names, both to find material relating to a particular film your star was in and star memorabilia in general. Less obvious searches, such as the director's name or the studio name, may produce hits on material that may be out of the mainstream but nonetheless interesting to a dedicated collector.

hold movie-memorabilia sales at their posh auction rooms. The more affordable replicas, both licensed and facsimile, may be found on auction sites such as eBay or on the studios' Web sites.

Since most of these items are facsimiles, it's crucial to know exactly what you're getting (an actual prop used in the production, a licensed replica, or a knockoff). Ask questions and get a detailed receipt with a clear return policy.

To learn more:

- Disney auctions on eBay: http://pages.ebay.com/disney/index.html
- Planet Hollywood auctions on eBay: www.planethollywood.com/auctions/frameset.htm
- Planet Hollywood Web site: www.planethollywood.com
- Universal Studios Web site: www.universalstudios.com
- eBay keywords: prop, star wars, costume
- eBay categories: Movies/Memorabilia
- *Everything You Need to Know About Star Wars Collectibles,* Brian Semling

What's the best strategy for bidding in an online auction?

Although some bidders like to open with the highest price they're willing to pay at the start of an auction (to discourage others from outbidding them), many bidders prefer to wait until the last possible moment before the auction's close to place their bid. This practice, called sniping, is considered unfair by some. It also runs the risk that your bid may not be executed before the auction clock runs out. Don't worry about entering bids to become the temporary top bidder over the course of the auction (usually five to ten days). The site will automatically execute interim bids up to your maximum.

Stagecoach, 1939, United Artists, "Rainbow" (final continuity) script. Signed by director John Ford and producer Walter Wanger, this script sold for $6,900 at a 1999 auction. Accompanying it was a letter from John LeRoy Johnson, director of publicity, to Ernest Haycox, author of the story "Stage to Lordsburg," on which the film was based. The letter reads in part, "Since the script is really our stock-in-trade one seldom ever leaves the studio, so you may feel complimented in possessing the only copy of 'Stagecoach' to leave the files." *Photo courtesy of Skinner, Inc.*

Woman of the Year, 1942, MGM, lobby card. In Spencer Tracy and Katharine Hepburn's first film together, both work for the same newspaper. This battle-of-the-sexes comedy set the standard for their twenty-five years as one of Hollywood's favorite romantic teams. When the two leads were introduced to each other by producer Joseph L. Mankiewicz, Hepburn, at five foot seven and wearing four-inch heels, quipped to her new co-star, "I'm afraid I'm a little tall for you, Mr. Tracy." "Don't worry, Miss Hepburn," Tracy answered quietly. "I'll cut you down to my size." *Photo courtesy of Michael B. King.*

What are seller reserve prices?

The reserve price is the lowest price that the seller is willing to accept for an item. This amount often isn't disclosed until the end of the auction. If the item reaches its reserve price, the site will indicate that the reserve is met and the item will be sold.

How does the transaction take place if I'm the winning bidder?

If you've placed the winning bid on an item, the site will notify both you and the seller by e-mail, and provide your e-mail addresses. Typically, the seller will send the successful bidder an e-mail message explaining shipping and payment options.

What if the item arrives and it isn't as described?

In that case, the seller should let you return it and refund your money. But if the item was correctly described and you're simply unhappy with it, you're probably stuck with it.

Should I post feedback?

When the transaction is complete, each party should post feedback into the other party's profile. If you made prompt payment and conducted yourself in a proper manner, the seller should give you positive feedback. If the seller described the item accurately, shipped it promptly and in sufficient packaging, and worked to resolve any disputes, then it's customary for you to give positive feedback. Negative feedback is a last resort reserved for instances in which all means to resolve a dispute have been tried with no satisfactory resolution.

What are the pros and cons of buying in a live auction?

In today's market, some of the very best items are sold at auctions that take place before a live audience. But competition can be fierce, as evidenced by the astronomical prices sometimes seen at these auctions. But just as every auction has items that sell for far too much, every auction also has its share of outright bargains. Be prepared and patient, and you'll find those bargains!

How do I find out about live auctions?

You'll find notices of movie-memorabilia auctions in the specialized trade publications listed in "Resources to Further Your Collecting" on pages 116–117. Local newspapers also list auctions in their classifieds.

What's the role of the auctioneer?

The auctioneer is the person who actually takes bids for the items. He or she will pick up or point to the item up for bid and briefly describe it. Auctioneers usually are paid a commission based on the final selling price, so it's to their advantage to get the highest possible price.

How should I prepare for a live auction?

Try to inspect any items you're interested in before the auction begins. Many auctions schedule preview periods, sometimes the day before or on the day of the auction. Previewing is especially crucial for expensive or rare items and at smaller auction houses that don't guarantee sales. If you can't look at an item in person, request a detailed written condition report. Don't assume that something must be in good condition just because it's being offered by a "legitimate" auction house.

Next, determine beforehand what you're willing to pay. This will help you avoid bidding more than the item's true market value. In arriving at your maximum, be sure to factor in any buyer's premium that may apply. This is a commission the auctioneer may charge the winning bidder (in addition to the commission he receives from the item's seller). If you do not have a reseller's tax identification number, the auction house will also charge you applicable state sales tax on top of your winning bid price. If the item will have to be shipped, get a shipping quote. Auction houses often have exclusive agreements with shippers that can add substantially to the final cost of the object. A collector-dealer we interviewed had to pay more than $300 for three lobby cards he won at a London auction to be shipped to the U.S.!

Finally, during the auction, be aware of what those around you are bidding. If someone you know to be a dealer is still bidding, there's a good chance the lot hasn't yet reached its true value, since a dealer probably wants it for resale. On the other hand, if a dealer is bidding on behalf of a client, he may bid up to top market value to secure the item. It pays to have done your homework beforehand and to know the history of prices paid for items comparable to the one you desire.

Is it difficult to register to bid at a live auction?

Not at all. You probably can even do it by mail. If you have a driver's license and a credit card, you're all set. Some auction houses also ask for credit and bank references if you plan to pay by check. You'll be assigned a bidder number, and at the more established houses, you'll be issued a paddle showing your number.

Exactly how does the bidding work at a live auction?

Some items may have reserve prices. The auctioneer will determine the opening bid based on this reserve and on any absentee bids received before the sale. Often, bidding will start at about half the item's "low estimate." For example, if it's expected to sell for between $600 and $1,000, the auctioneer may start the bidding at around $300.

Then, as bids come in, the bid price will escalate—usually in increments appropriate to the amount bid. For instance, if the amount bid is between $100 and $500, the increment may be $10; when the bidding reaches $500, the increment may be increased to $25. Once the bidding has topped out and the auctioneer receives no further bids, he'll close the bidding, usually with the words "Fair warning; going once; going twice; sold." If you happen to be the successful bidder, you show your paddle or call out your bid number. In the event that the bidding doesn't reach the reserve price, the auctioneer pulls the item (called "passing") and it's not sold.

Breakfast at Tiffany's, 1961, Paramount, insert. This insert sold for $1,840 at a 1999 auction. *Photo courtesy of Skinner, Inc.*

Can I still bid on items if I can't be present at the auction?

Yes, indeed. It's always best to bid in person, but if you can't be present, you can preregister and submit bids for all items you're interested in. Your bid may have to be higher than a certain percentage of the low estimate. Once the auction is under way, your bid will be executed as if you were there.

An even better strategy is to bid by phone, which lets you participate live in the auction. However, you should still set your maximums and go no further by phone than you would have in person. Established auction houses have several phone lines manned by staff who will call you when your desired lot comes up and will stay on the line with you during bidding, acting as your proxy in placing bids.

What's involved in claiming my winnings?

You may pick up the items you win at the auction house or, in many cases, have them shipped to you. Shipping policies are usually specified in the registration agreement; by signing the agreement, you agree to abide by those policies. Don't even think of not honoring your winning bid. When you bid, you enter a legal contract to purchase the item at the agreed price, and you'll be held to it. And remember, once the gavel drops and you've won an item, legal title transfers to you. Any damage or loss after that is your responsibility—unless the piece is damaged while being removed from the podium.

Star Wars

From the beginning, with the opening of the first *Star Wars* film in 1977, Lucasfilms merchandised the picture perhaps more extensively than any before it. Having painstakingly pioneered many of the special effects, George Lucas's team reaped the rewards of their innovations by translating them—or licensing others to translate them—into thousands of stylishly accessorized action figures, vehicles, play sets, weapons, cereal boxes, games, clothing items, pins, trading cards, and more, all of which were eagerly gobbled up by consumers of all ages.

The array of *Star Wars* items on eBay is daunting. They may be found by searching under Toys>Action Figures>Star Wars, which will bring up the General, Vintage (1977–89), NeoClassic (1989–99), and Prequels (1999–present) categories. You'll also find them on the Sci-Fi theme page. You can find trading cards by searching Collectibles>Trading Card>Science Fiction>Star Wars. Or, you can just type in your particular interest, such as "R2D2." You'll turn up items like the R2D2 figural telephone, which sold recently for $30; the figural Pepsi cooler in less-than-perfect condition, $100; and the 3¾" figure from 1977, with no package, at $6. Typing in "Star Destroyer" will yield items like a vintage Star Destroyer commander, mint on card, for $36; a die-cast Star Destroyer executor, mint on card, at $21; and a rare POTF2 Super Star Destroyer, mint in box with one dent on top, for $76. You can spend days surfing for *Star Wars* memorabilia!

Since the range of *Star Wars* collectibles is tremendous, the beginning collector should concentrate on just one area. Find a favorite character, a type of collectible, or a particular film. Start with the least expensive items while you're learning your way around the field. Since there are many unlicensed items on the market, be sure you can tell the difference and that what you buy is priced appropriately. Your best protection is to do your homework and buy only from a trusted dealer who will give you an itemized written receipt. When searching on eBay, type your choice into the search box and specify "the exact phrase." And remember, any item without accessories and packaging is worth far less than one with both.

As part of your education, check out the online *Star Wars* collectibles newsletter maintained by Brian Semling, who also runs Brian's Toys, a site devoted to *Star Wars* toys.

To learn more:

- *Everything You Need to Know About Star Wars Collectibles,* Brian Semling
- Brian's *Star Wars* Newsletter: www.egroups.com/group/brianstoys
- Brian's Toys Web site: www.brianstoys.com
- *Hake's Price Guide to Character Toy Premiums,* Ted Hake
- *O'Brien's Collecting Toys,* Elizabeth Stephan, editor

Star Wars, 1977, Twentieth Century Fox, half-sheet, Style A.
This variation of the more familiar design sold for $2,300
at a 1999 auction. *Photo courtesy of Skinner, Inc.*

A Ground-Floor Opportunity: "Coming Attractions" Glass Slides

The forerunner of today's 35 mm slide, the magic lantern glass slide (measuring 3¼" x 4") was introduced in the early days of photography. Glass slides were pressed into service in theaters of the vaudeville era to urge courteous behavior: "Please remove your hat" and "Do not spit on the floor." They also were used to advertise the products of local merchants (some multiplex cinemas use 35 mm slides the same way today).

With the advent of projected moving pictures, glass slides kept the audience entertained before the show and during reel changes. Slides announcing coming attractions reached their zenith during the era of silent films, though they continued to be produced into the 1950s. Tinted by hand, and featuring a blank space at the bottom for the projectionist to fill in the upcoming show dates, these slides have the look of stained glass. They re-create the excitement of the movies' beginnings: the first studios, the birth of the star system, and the revolution of sound. Their graphic styles range from the stately neoclassical to Art Nouveau and Art Deco. Inspired by technology and the machine age, the latter style announces: "It's an all-talking picture!" Is it any wonder these slides are becoming irresistible to collectors?

Today, coming-attractions glass slides, particularly those from the silent era, are hot collectibles. In the case of some films, such as Erich von Stroheim's legendary lost *The Devil's Passkey,* released in 1919 by Universal, slides may be the only artifacts to survive. The chances of finding a title card or half-sheet poster from many silent classics are slim indeed, but glass slides advertising them can be found, sometimes in two or more styles, and at prices well below what one would pay for a poster from the same title, if it were available.

Among the most sought-after stars "under glass" is Clara Bow, especially after she made *It* (Paramount, 1927) and became an icon for the liberated woman of the flapper era. Then there's that other liberated woman of the period, Joan Crawford, whose background as a prizewinning Charleston dancer served her well in *Dance Fools Dance* (MGM, 1931). Greta Garbo's last silent film for MGM, *A Woman of Affairs* (1929), is noteworthy because, although her name is above the title, she's billed after her costar, John Gilbert. It was the last time *that* would happen!

A Paramount Picture

CLARA BOW
'HULA'
CLIVE BROOK
A VICTOR FLEMING
PRODUCTION

Hula, 1927, Paramount, image from a glass slide. In this romantic drama Clara Bow plays Hula Calhoun, wild-child daughter of a pineapple plantation owner. Salacious treats like *Hula*'s risqué bathing scenes temporarily disappeared from Hollywood films after the adoption of the Motion Picture Production Code in 1930, which strove to banish—or at least limit—indecency and immorality. *Photo courtesy of Michael B. King.*

Glass slides can be found at movie-memorabilia shows, such as Cinefest in Syracuse, New York, and on auction sites, such as eBay. You're not likely to discover them at an antiques shop or flea market. As is true for posters, slides from classic horror, science-fiction, and fantasy films bring the highest prices. A glass slide from *Metropolis* (UFA/Paramount, 1926) recently sold for $1,300 on eBay. Lon Chaney *Phantom of the Opera* and Charlie Chaplin *Gold Rush* slides sold for $500 each; others range in price from $30 to $300.

Unlike posters and stills, which could be tacked up on a wall and enjoyed long after the film's run had ended, most glass slides were discarded after use. Of those that were saved, many became damaged over time, being extremely fragile and highly susceptible to emulsion deterioration. Not surprisingly, then, condition is a major consideration. Even a broken or chipped slide may be worth keeping if the graphics are intact or if it still has its cardboard frame, which can be pried off and reattached to a desirable piece that's missing its frame.

Displaying glass slides isn't as difficult as you might think. Collectors who don't happen to have a magic lantern handy can mount slides in the glass doors of cupboards, with a light fixed to illuminate them from behind. Or, you can adapt light boxes, available at art-supply stores. After removing the clear glass plate from the top of the unit, place the slides on the frosted glass underneath, then cover them with a sheet of clear acrylic glazing, such as Plexiglas. Choose the type that screens out ultraviolet light. Secure the top sheet with wood screws and ordinary frame molding. The box can then be hung on a wall to display your slides to advantage.

Light boxes use fluorescent tubes, which do not generate much heat. If you're using incandescent fixtures, use low-wattage bulbs—such as the tubular kind for curio cabinets and frame-mounted picture lights. Excessive heat may cause degradation because expansion in the glass may crack or "spider" the emulsion of the image; for this reason, halogen bulbs should not be used. As always with photographic materials, it's best to limit the time the lights are on to when you're actually viewing the slides. Finally, display your slides well away from direct sunlight.

Photo Gallery

It Happened One Night, 1934, Columbia, jumbo lobby card. The first film to take all the high-profile Academy Awards, *It Happened One Night* won best picture, best director (Frank Capra), best actor (Clark Gable), and best actress (Claudette Colbert). This card sold at auction for $2,530 in 1999. *Photo courtesy of Skinner, Inc.*

This Gun For Hire, 1942, Paramount, one-sheet. This noir favorite, featuring the winning combination of beautiful blonde and double-crossed tough guy, launched Alan Ladd's career. Collectors consider this one of the most desirable posters from the 1940s. *Photo courtesy of Michael B. King.*

▶ *The Mummy,* 1932, Universal Studios, one-sheet. Only two copies of this poster are known to exist. Illustrated by Karoly Grosz, Universal's advertising art director in the '30s, this gorgeous poster realized a record $453,500 in a 1997 auction. *Photo courtesy of Sotheby's (Todd Feiertag Collection auction).*

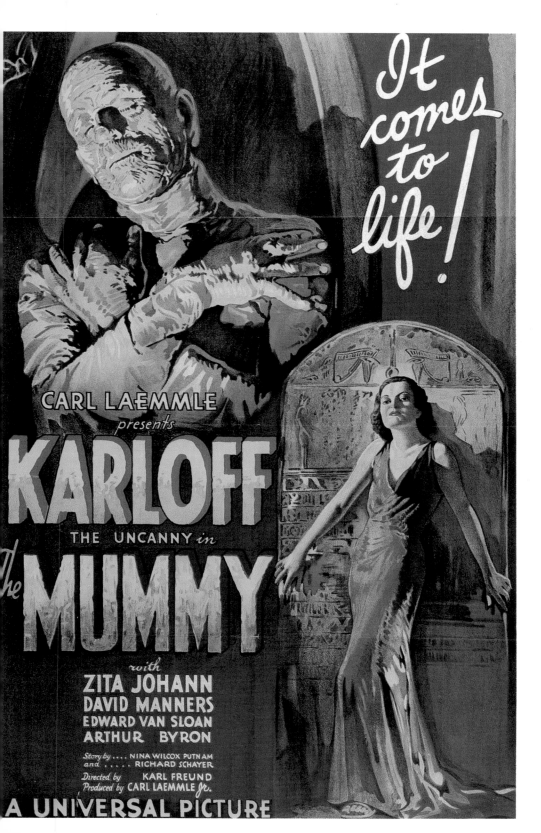

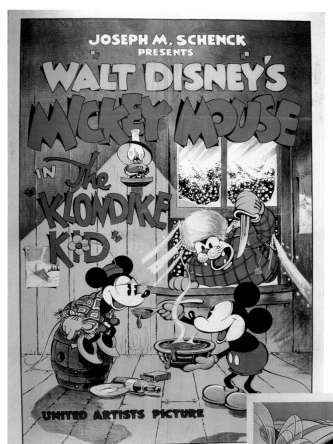

The Klondike Kid, 1932, United Artists, one-sheet. The ever-popular Mickey Mouse holds high appeal for collectors. This poster sold for $57,500 at a 1995 Christie's auction. *Photo courtesy of Michael B. King.*

Pinocchio, 1940, RKO, one-sheet. Disney Studios' posters were as colorful as the Technicolor animated classics they advertised. *Photo courtesy of Sotheby's (Todd Feiertag Collection auction).*

Painted Post, 1929, one-sheet. This iconic image publicized cowboy star Tom Mix's last film for William Fox before he moved to the F.B.O. studio. Mix made more than three hundred Westerns, but the arrival of talkies finished his film career. *Photo courtesy of Michael B. King.*

The Dawn Rider, 1935, Monogram, one-sheet. While not one of John Wayne's better-remembered films, *Dawn Rider*'s early place in his work and the dynamic stone-litho graphics make this poster desirable. *Photo courtesy of Michael B. King.*

Lost Horizon, 1937, Columbia, six-sheet. This is the only known copy of this remarkable poster. It was illustrated by James Montgomery Flagg, designer of the world-famous 1917 Uncle Sam "I Want You for U.S. Army" poster. *Photo courtesy of Sotheby's (Todd Feiertag Collection auction).*

Angel, 1937, Paramount, one-sheet. The mesmerizing Marlene Dietrich probably accounts for the sale price of $4,025 in 1999 for this poster—critics generally consider the film disappointing while collectors treasure the poster. *Photo courtesy of Skinner, Inc.*

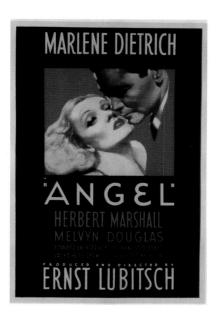

The Postman Always Rings Twice, 1946, MGM, one-sheet. A collector paid $2,875 in 1999 for this poster; the film has been called a prototype for today's "erotic thrillers." The black background is unusual for MGM. *Photo courtesy of Skinner, Inc.*

Casablanca, 1942, Warner Bros., insert. With its unforgettable characters and highly quotable lines, *Casablanca* is thought by many to be Hollywood's greatest movie. *Photo courtesy of Todd Feiertag.*

▶ *Metropolis*, 1926, UFA/Paramount, glass slide. Fritz Lang's astonishing vision of a futuristic city and its mechanized society, considered the summit of German Expressionist filmmaking, is perfectly captured in this piece. *Photo courtesy of Michael B. King.*

Blonde Venus, 1932, Paramount, lobby card. Desperate to provide expensive medical care for her husband, Marlene Dietrich's Helen Faraday submits to an affair with wealthy playboy Nick Townsend, played by Cary Grant. This card conveys the exoticism of the Dietrich–Josef von Sternberg collaborations. *Photo courtesy of Michael B. King.*

Citizen Kane, 1941, RKO, scene card. A constant favorite with critics, *Citizen Kane* won Orson Welles and Herman J. Mankiewicz the best-original-screenplay Oscar. This card, showing Welles (as Kane) delivering his gubernatorial speech before his giant portrait, is highly prized by collectors. *Photo courtesy of Michael B. King.*

The Petrified Forest, 1936, Warner Bros., lobby card. The screen version of Robert E. Sherwood's hit play is best known as the film which catapulted Humphrey Bogart to fame in his role as a gangster. Here Bette Davis, an aspiring writer working as a waitress in a remote service-station café in the Arizona desert, comforts wandering idealist Leslie Howard after he has been shot by Bogart. Ensemble acting by the Warner Bros. stock company at its best. *Photo courtesy of Michael B. King.*

Vertigo, 1958, Paramount, half-sheet. One of Alfred Hitchcock's best, *Vertigo* is regarded by some as a revealing look into the director's psyche. James Stewart plays Scottie Ferguson, whose obsessive desire to mold a woman into his ideal seems to mirror Hitchcock's own tendency to remake his leading actresses. The stunning graphic design is by Saul Bass. *Photo courtesy of Michael B. King.*

The Searchers, 1956, Warner Bros., lobby card. In what many consider his finest performance, John Wayne portrays racist Civil War veteran Ethan Edwards, a man who may want to punish as much as protect the niece who was kidnapped by Comanches. *Photo courtesy of Michael B. King.*

59

Singin' in the Rain, 1952, MGM, one-sheet. Perhaps the most entertaining of all movie musicals. When asked to create a plot that would weave together numbers based on MGM's musical output over the years, screenwriters Adolph Green and Betty Comden found that the best of the tunes appeared in the "all talking all singing" Hollywood musicals of the late '20s, and chose this tumultuous period of transition from silents to talkies as their setting. The art of this one-sheet captures the exuberant ambience. *Photo courtesy of Michael B. King.*

The Wizard of Oz, 1939, MGM, lobby card. No movie exerts a greater continuing fascination for collectors. *Photo courtesy of Sotheby's (Todd Feiertag Collection auction).*

Shall We Dance, 1937, RKO, title lobby card and three scene cards. Fred Astaire and Ginger Rogers sparkle in this Gershwin musical, as do the wonderful Art Deco graphics of these pieces. *Photo courtesy of Sotheby's (Todd Feiertag Collection auction).*

Gold Diggers of 1933, Warner Bros., half-sheet. Chorus girls capture the hearts of wealthy men in this Depression-era musical. The charming opening number features Ginger Rogers singing "We're in the Money"—in pig Latin. *Photo courtesy of Michael B. King.*

Animal Crackers, 1930, Paramount, lobby card. Chico and Harpo ham it up in the Marx Brothers' second movie, which features members of the original Broadway cast. *Photo courtesy of Michael B. King.*

King Kong, 1933, RKO, three-sheet, Style B. Perhaps the greatest (and tenderest) monster movie ever made, *King Kong* still thrills with its innovative stop-action animation sequences. Only four copies of this poster are known to exist. One of them sold for $70,700 at a 1998 auction. *Photo courtesy of Skinner, Inc.*

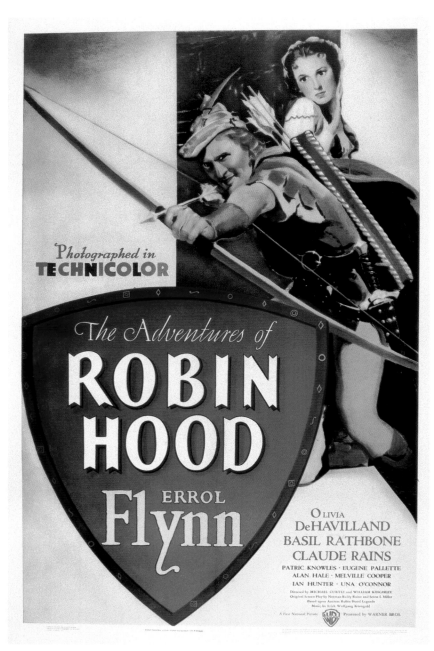

The Adventures of Robin Hood, 1938, Warner Bros., one-sheet. Warner Bros.' answer to the censorship restrictions imposed in the mid-'30s was to revive the historical adventure film. The twenty-nine-year-old Errol Flynn was at his swashbuckling best in this lavish spectacle, a stunning example of Technicolor cinematography. *Photo courtesy of Sotheby's (Todd Feiertag Collection auction).*

NOW THAT YOU'RE READY TO START COLLECTING

When experienced collectors go shopping, they take along much more than their checkbook. These tools can help you evaluate items you find and then transport them safely home if you decide to make them yours.

The Collector's Toolbox

- **Tape measure.** Since movie posters come in standard sizes, and since the odd sizes of reproductions can give them away, a tape measure is especially handy for the novice collector.
- **Black light.** Holding a black light close to the surface of a poster will let you see areas of restoration, wear, or tampering not visible under ordinary light.
- **Notepad and pen.** When you come across an item that the owner isn't quite ready to sell (or you're not quite ready to buy), jot down a description of it and the dealer's contact information for future reference.
- **Tote bag**. A tote bag can come in handy for transporting smaller objects such as lobby cards and folded posters.
- **Stiff cardboard, utility knife, and tape.** Sandwich posters between sheets of stiff cardboard (or foam core) cut to size

with a utility knife and taped securely. Some collectors prefer to roll posters in cardboard shipping tubes.

- **Camera.** A camera is handy for documenting posters or where you found them. A digital camera lets you view your images as you shoot, and lets you store them on your computer.
- **Magnifying glass.** This can be helpful in reading the small print and dates at the bottom of posters, and also in determining whether a poster was printed on an offset press or by stone lithography.
- **Your want list.** Make sure it includes your name, address (if you use a post-office box), phone number, and e-mail address. Group the items on your want list by category, and try to keep it short so dealers can scan it quickly.
- *Poster Price Almanac,* **John Kisch, editor.** Last but certainly not least, this price guide will enable you to see what specific posters have sold for recently.

What Determines the Value of a Movie Poster?

Initially, finding posters you'd like to add to your collection is relatively easy. As you become more seasoned, finding the most desirable ones in desirable condition at the right price takes more work. But that's a large part of the thrill of the hunt. Each of the following attributes has some impact on a poster's value—and therefore on the price you'll pay.

Condition

Unless a poster has already been restored or simply was never used, you're likely to find tack holes, tears, pieces missing, writing, tape, or stains. But if the poster is rare enough, these defects may be tolerable.

To find any posters older than, say, forty years in mint condition is rare indeed. A three-sheet or six-sheet poster will have been stored folded, but if the only fold lines are the original ones and the poster is otherwise free of wear, it may still be considered mint.

Mint condition for lobby cards is unused, either individually or in complete sets of eight, and in the original envelope if a complete set. Mint-condition window cards are in their original

14" x 22" size, free of folds, and with the blank area at the top not trimmed away. Most collectors don't mind if the name of the theater or some other message has been written in at the top; in fact, some think it adds to the card's appeal when framed.

Damage. It's a fact of life—movie posters are made of paper, one of the most fragile materials known to man, and one that's susceptible to a wide range of damage.

- **Normal usage wear.** Normal usage wear for a poster includes tack holes, small tears, small tape repairs on the back, an extra fold or two, and other minor blemishes that can befall paper over time.
- **Unusual usage wear.** Unusual usage wear on a poster includes major stains, large pieces missing, tape that's bled through to the front, writing on the front, insect damage, and other major signs of use.
- **Water or humidity.** Exposure to water or excessive humidity can be disastrous. Warping, stains, and eventually mold or mildew can result.
- **Sunlight.** Prolonged exposure to direct sunlight can fade the pigments on a poster, making it look washed out and drastically reducing its value.
- **Grease or oil.** These stains can be almost impossible to remove. If they're still visible even after restoration, the value of the poster will plummet.
- **Deterioration due to acid in the paper.** The paper on which posters were, and still are, printed was not intended to last for the ages. Thus, yellowing and brittleness due to acid in the paper are commonplace among posters yet to be rescued by dealers and collectors. Once a valuable poster has been recognized, having it treated by a professional restorer with a deacidifying bath, plus having it backed with archival paper and linen, may arrest this deterioration.
- **Scratches, dents, gouges, tears, and punctures.** The older and rarer the poster, the more forgivable these problems become. Also, the more confined they are to the border and peripheral areas, the better.

- **Rodents.** You may find signs that rats or mice have nibbled away at a folded poster.
- **Insects.** Insects such as silverfish can cause significant damage to posters by eating through the paper or by marring the surface.

Popeye and Olive Oil

A poster-collector friend of ours is able to laugh about this now, but when it occurred it was a minor tragedy. "Years ago, I bought a *Popeye* poster [from a 1940 cartoon short] and had it mailed to me. Apparently, somewhere in the postal system a container of olive oil broke open onto a lot of mail, including my poster. It soaked through the heavy packaging and stained the poster. I had to have it restored, but even after that you could still see the stains."

When you're able to buy a poster in person, take the time to examine it carefully for damage. More often, you'll be buying a poster sight unseen from a mail-order dealer or over the Internet. In these cases, always ask the seller, "Exactly what's keeping this piece from being in mint condition?" Put the burden on the seller to tell you everything that's wrong with it.

Missing or replaced parts. There are no mechanical parts to movie posters, of course, but pieces can still be missing. Perhaps part of the poster remained stapled to the wall when it was removed. Or some of the paper may have worn or been eaten away along a fold line. In the case of a three-sheet or larger poster that came in multiple sections, one of the sections could be missing.

A thumbnail-size piece missing from a blank border is easily restored. Similarly, a piece of archival tape can fix a hairline tear along a fold line. But larger problems are less acceptable. Even though it may be possible to restore the missing piece, it could be costly. As a rule, it's much better to spend more up front on a poster in better condition than to buy an example that's in lesser condition with the intent of restoring it.

Repairs and restoration. With delicate movie paper, there's a fine line between simple preservation and restoration. For example, it's a routine practice to back one-sheet, three-sheet, and six-sheet posters with linen. The paper is first cleaned, deacidified, and affixed to thin archival paper, then mounted on a sheet of linen, leaving about an inch of linen showing around the edges. Even posters that are in mint condition are routinely linen-backed, though our experts disagree about whether this is necessary. Materials printed on heavier stock, such as half-sheets, window cards, inserts, and lobby cards, may also be backed, but with paper rather than linen. Under no circumstances should any piece be laminated in plastic or dry-mounted on a stiff material such as foam core.

As far as repairs are concerned, most collectors are very accepting of professional restoration of tears, small missing pieces, pinholes, and removal of tape, dirt, and stains. Since many poster repairs are made on the back, on an unbacked poster they're easy to detect: just turn the poster over.

With backed posters, however, it can sometimes be almost impossible to detect restoration under regular lighting. Try using a black light, if one is available. Otherwise, try shining a strong light through the poster from back to front to spot any areas where pieces may have been replaced. Variations in the texture or sheen of the surface may indicate in-painting or touch-ups with colored pencil. When an entire border has been repainted (often done to even out color and texture when pieces have been replaced), you'll notice a slight difference in thickness.

Is the Glass Half-Empty or Half-Full?

How do you decide whether to pass on a poster that's incomplete or to buy it and spend more money restoring it? Much depends on how rare or expensive it is. For example, if you found a poster for the Robert De Niro film *Meet the Parents* and 25 percent of it was missing, you definitely should pass it by. It would be easy to find another one in mint condition. But if you found an original Boris Karloff *Frankenstein* poster with 25 percent missing, consider it your lucky day. Since only four or five examples are known to exist, this would be a rare find indeed and well worth purchasing for restoration. That is, if you can afford it. A *Frankenstein* one-sheet in pristine condition sold in 1993 for the tidy sum of $198,000.

Once you've examined many posters firsthand, you'll begin to recognize signs of repair. In the meantime, always ask sellers to explain what's been done to any poster you're interested in buying. If you're buying by mail, make sure the seller will refund your money if you're not happy with your purchase.

Original Packaging

The only original packaging that pertains to movie paper is the printed envelope usually made of brown paper used for complete sets of lobby cards or stills from the 1920s through the early 1970s. These envelopes are rare, but though they would enhance the value of a set, it wouldn't be by much.

Original Labeling

Even though posters bear no applied labels or stickers per se, sometimes the lithographer's name is printed directly on the poster. For those who collect posters from specific lithographers, this identification can be a value-enhancing addition.

Intrinsic Characteristics

Of the many factors that contribute to a poster's value, the one that trumps them all is image quality. After all, posters are visual media. When you match a fantastic-looking poster with a major star and film, you have everything! The poster for *The Mummy* that sold at Sotheby's on March 1, 1997, for a record-breaking $453,500 is a perfect example. Besides being one of only two known examples, it's a knockout of a poster. Or take the Style A three-sheet for *King Kong* that depicts the giant ape perched atop the Empire State Building being dive-bombed by biplane fighters. That poster, of which only a handful are known to exist, sold at Sotheby's in April 1999 for $244,500. The image has left an indelible impression on millions of movie watchers for generations. It has attained the status of a cultural icon.

In determining the value of a poster, next in importance after image quality is renown of the artist. Posters for *How to Murder Your Wife,* designed by Charles Addams—or for the German film *Querelle,* by Andy Warhol—are simply more valuable and collectible because of who designed them.

Age

The age of a poster doesn't necessarily dictate its value. There are many posters from the 1960s that are worth much more than posters from the 1920s. One of the reasons, of course, is that most people today don't remember the stars from eighty years ago, but they do remember the stars from the films they grew up watching.

When a poster actually bears a date, it's usually placed somewhere on the lower border. It might be in Arabic or Roman numerals. Twentieth Century Fox usually used Roman numerals on its posters, for example.

Sometimes you will find the last two digits of the film's year followed by a slash and another number (such as 51/245). When the second number is larger than the first, many people assume incorrectly that it indicates poster number 51 out of 245, the system used on numbered editions. In fact, the first number indicates that the poster is from 1951; the second number is the studio or printer's designation for the film (it sometimes indicates that this is the 245th film released that year). It has nothing to do with how many posters were produced. If there is an *R* in front of the number, the film was being rereleased that year; the poster isn't an original issue.

If a poster isn't dated, there are other ways to determine its age. Check to see what releasing company is mentioned on the poster. Many times, if a poster isn't from the original release but from a rerelease, a different releasing company will be listed, either by itself or with the original company. Another clue is if the name of the lithographer is printed on the poster. Many of these companies

My Fair Lady, 1964, Warner Bros., one-sheet. With twelve nominations and eight wins at the Academy Awards, *My Fair Lady* is one of the most successful musical romances— yet in it, famously, no one ever gets kissed. *Photo courtesy of Chisholm-Larsson Gallery.*

Autographs

A movie-star autograph is a collector's prize—a way to "own a piece" of one's idol. What could be more personal than a star's name, created by his or her own hand? How thrilling it would be to possess an autograph book filled with the signatures of film greats such as Marilyn Monroe, the Marx Brothers, and Charlie Chaplin!

The best sources for movie-star autographs are the stars themselves, signing in person, right before your eyes. That's why autograph hunters line the sidewalk entrances to restaurants-of-the-moment in major cities across the U.S. and Europe, and haunt film locations everywhere. A bonus: these collectibles are free! Most stars will graciously sign almost any piece of paper, if asked politely. If you don't happen to live near a big city, you can buy autographs from a reputable dealer, one who will give you a detailed written receipt and who will provide a full refund if the item is ever found to be a fake.

Prices for star autographs range from a few dollars to thousands, depending on the magnitude of the star's fame and the object that's signed. The signatures of major stars who are deceased command the highest prices. Signatures on objects like paper napkins or menus are worth less than those on letters (especially handwritten ones), contracts, wills, or other personal items. A bank check signed by Marilyn Monroe will fetch about $1,500 at auction, but the autographed photo of a young star like Pauly Shore sells for only five bucks. Sometimes the value of an autograph on a scrap of paper can be enhanced by displaying it in a frame along with a photo of the star.

were around only for a short time (for example, Miner Litho Company didn't produce posters after the 1930s). The definitive source for dating movie paper is the film's press book, also called the exhibitor campaign book or bally book, which pictures all the different sizes of posters and lobby cards that made up the film's publicity campaign.

Rarity

The posters for many movies are rare—there are cases where no examples have been found of certain sizes known to have been printed. For the 1932 movie *The Mummy*, there are only three known one-sheets—one of the first style and two of the second style. One three-sheet and one window card are also known, but

Fakes and forgeries abound in the celebrity-autograph market. Thousands—perhaps millions—of autographs are available for sale on the Internet at auction sites such as eBay and Yahoo, both of which have celebrity-autograph categories, but the sites are unable to police their sellers. Individual dealers who obtain autographs themselves and who offer money-back certificates of authenticity are a safer bet. There also are Web rings of individual dealers that anyone can visit. Be sure to investigate ring members and their return policies thoroughly before making a purchase. Beginning collectors should seek out dealers who are members of organizations such as the Universal Autograph Collectors Club, which have clearly worded codes of ethics. Remember: When buying online, always ask questions about authenticity and return policies, and save the e-mail responses you get from the dealer. Don't buy from any dealer who refuses to answer all of your questions.

Autograph Collector magazine maintains a Web site that's updated frequently, presenting monthly columns, articles, news of the latest fakes and forgeries, and a feature called "Ask the Experts," where you can obtain advice on everything from values to caring for your collection.

To learn more:
- Alfie's Autographs of Hollywood: www.alfies.com
- Celebrity Autograph Collector's Ring: www.nav.webring.yahoo.com/hub?ring=autograph&list
- Universal Autograph Collectors Club: www.uacc.org/index.html
- *Autograph Collector* magazine: www.autographs.com/acm.htm

no inserts, half-sheets, or six-sheets. Another horror classic, James Whale's 1935 *The Bride of Frankenstein,* considered by many the greatest horror film of all time, had a huge publicity campaign that included a multitude of posters. Alas (for everyone in the collecting world other than its owner), only one example of a one-sheet poster from this movie is known to exist!

Rare production variations and anomalies do exist, usually in older stone-litho posters where a color was left out during the printing process. If anything, this decreases value, because most collectors want a poster printed the way it was intended.

The press book is the key to the style variants among posters for a particular film. A film may have had different one-sheet posters using different images, thus giving the theater owner some latitude in how to present the film to his clientele. Variants were generally given a letter—Style A, Style B, etc.—but studios sometimes intermingled codes (for instance, Styles C and D might designate variations for a poster of different size than Styles A and B). The original press book is the only definitive guide to what was actually produced and distributed to theaters (see "Bally Books and Press Kits" on pages 84–87 for more on press books).

Attribution

If a well-known artist such as Alberto Vargas, George Petty, Norman Rockwell, or Saul Bass produced the artwork for a poster, this adds to its value. Artist James Montgomery Flagg's Style D one-sheet for *Lost Horizon* recently sold for just under $22,000. Al Hirschfeld's Style C one-sheet for *Cabin in the Sky* brought just over $10,000. Not only are these artists renowned, but the posters they produced are exceptional. Many times, the signature of the artist appears as part of the artwork.

Cabin in the Sky, 1943, MGM, one-sheet. Vincente Minnelli's musical—rare in that it features an all-black cast but is not a revue—showcases Ethel Waters, Lena Horne, and Louis Armstrong.
Photo courtesy of Todd Feiertag.

Niagara, 1953, Twentieth Century Fox, one-sheet. This noir thriller gave Marilyn Monroe her first star break as the woman who plans to murder her mentally unstable husband (Joseph Cotton) while vacationing at Niagara Falls. The poster presents Monroe as a force of nature rivaling the falls itself. In this film Monroe takes "the longest walk in film history" as the camera follows her down a sidewalk in a tracking shot to infinity. Despite the murderous impulses of her character, Monroe's beauty and vulnerability evoke our sympathy to the very end. *Photo courtesy of Michael B. King.*

Doors to the Past

A collector we spoke with told us about a half-sheet from the Marilyn Monroe movie *Niagara* which he discovered had an interesting provenance. The poster was exceptionally bright, unfolded, and had no tears or pinholes, and so the collector had no problem with the price that the dealer was asking. But, as he later recalled, "only in a conversation I had with him about three months later did he happen to mention that this poster used to belong to Jim Morrison of the Doors and that [the dealer] had personally purchased it from Ray Manzarek, the Doors' keyboardist. Morrison had given Ray his posters before moving to France, where he subsequently died. So you could say that this *Niagara* poster was not only a piece of Marilyn Monroe history but a Doors collectible as well!"

Provenance

Is the value of a poster enhanced simply because a celebrated person owned it in the past? Even though there are several celebrities who collect movie posters—Martin Scorsese, Whoopi Goldberg, Nicholas Cage, Michael Jackson, Ron Howard, and Kirk Hammett, lead guitarist from Metallica, to name a few—provenance seems to have little impact on poster value. Great posters are great in their own right. They stand on their own.

Dealing with Reproductions, Fakes, and Reissues

As far back as the 1960s and 1970s, there were companies producing reproductions of movie posters. Among them were Portal Publications and Poflake Productions, which manufactured posters for such popular films as *Frankenstein* and *King Kong.* These were clearly identified as reproductions; the company names were plainly printed on the bottom borders. But thirty and forty years later, dealers and collectors get phone calls from people who say they have a rare original *Frankenstein* poster and think it's worth a fortune. They say it must be original because their grandmother had it in her basement for the last thirty years. Convincing these people that all they have is an old reproduction, worth very little, is sometimes easier said than done!

Should collectors ever consider buying a reproduction? That depends. Most people can never hope to afford an original poster from *The Mummy,* even if one of the few in existence were ever to be offered for sale. Reproductions of "the world's most expensive poster" are readily available, however. There's nothing wrong with displaying a reproduction of a spectacular poster, as long as you realize that's all it is.

Fakes are more difficult to spot, because their intent is to deceive. Still, the movie-poster field is new enough that there are few instances of fakes being offered for sale. One notable exception was a fake set of lobby cards from the Beatles film *A Hard Day's Night* that turned up for sale at a very low price. Upon close inspection, it could be seen that the "pinholes" in the corners of the cards were actually just photographic reproductions of the pinholes on an original set.

A Hard Day's Night, 1964, United Artists, one-sheet. Director Richard Lester accompanied Beatles songs with quick-cut montages, and a new style of moviemaking was born. This witty, merry romp enjoyed a successful rerelease in 2000. *Photo courtesy of Sotheby's (Todd Feiertag Collection auction).*

Reissues (or rereleases, as they're sometimes called) fall somewhere between original-release posters and reproductions, in both cost and availability. That's because reissues, authorized by studios to promote films when they were being put into theaters for a second run, are still a piece of movie history, and they are original movie posters. Reproductions are printed in much larger numbers specifically to sell to fans—perhaps long after a film's theatrical release. As such, they're at best a *picture* of a piece of movie history. Reissued movie paper is a wonderful alternative for collectors who got into the hobby late or who can't afford original issues. Some rereleases even contain images that are different than those on the originals—and in some cases superior to the originals— and thus have become sought-after collectibles in their own right.

Because most of the signs that distinguish original movie paper from reissues and reproductions involve their printing and manufacture, please refer to the "Materials and Manufacture" section of "Essential Background on Movie Memorabilia" (pages 21–22). And be especially careful when you see "reprints" offered for sale. They may be mere reproductions and not legitimate reissues. Especially when you're buying through the mail, always ask the seller if the piece was actually used to promote the film in theaters. And make sure you have full return privileges if you're not satisfied with your purchase.

Building Your Collection

Most novice poster collectors walk a tightrope. Their newfound interest and growing knowledge of the field are propelling them into the market, but they still have questions about everything from what to buy to how to care for their pieces once they own them. If this sounds like you, take heart. Here's expert advice from collectors who've walked in your shoes.

2001: A Space Odyssey, 1968, MGM, six-sheet. This poster for Stanley Kubrick's sci-fi masterpiece sold for $1,035 at a 1999 auction. *Photo courtesy of Skinner, Inc.*

Production still from *Schindler's List*, 1993, Universal. A winner of seven Academy Awards, this film tells the story of Oskar Schindler, a businessman who saved the lives of more than one thousand Polish Jews during the Holocaust. Director Steven Spielberg (at left) fought with Universal to make the film in black-and-white. *Photo courtesy of Michael B. King.*

How do I decide what to collect?

First, collect whatever you like best. Most collectors focus on a specific movie star (such as Marilyn Monroe), film genre (film noir), or director (Alfred Hitchcock). For others, size matters (they may collect only half-sheets or lobby cards). Still other collectors seek out only posters that depict certain objects, such as trains, cameras, or parachutes.

Do most people look only for the "crown jewels," or do they collect more broadly?

Actually, they do both. For example, the crown jewel of one advanced collection is an original six-sheet (remember, that's a whopping 81" x 81") of the 1932 film *White Zombie* starring Bela Lugosi. It's probably the only one in existence. With a centerpiece like that, if you wanted to continue buying movie posters at all, you'd have no choice but to relax your standards!

79

Citizen Kane, 1941, RKO, souvenir program. This forty-page program, a reminder of the firestorm that surrounded the release of Orson Welles's masterpiece, sold for $1,610 at a 1999 auction. *Photo courtesy of Skinner, Inc.*

Paper Collectibles and Ephemera

Items meant to be thrown away have always been popular collectibles simply because their disposability presumably increases their rarity. But as public enthusiasm for collecting grew, so did the number of items saved by those who believed their value would increase over time. Consequently, paper items and ephemera are some of the more plentiful and affordable memorabilia in the field.

This category includes programs from film-related events, movie magazines, maps to stars' homes, calendars, sheet music, trading cards, comic books, ads for films and for products endorsed by film stars, scrapbooks, paper dolls, and other items with stars' images on them.

Souvenir programs from the Academy Awards ceremonies sell in the $20 to $50 range, and movie-premiere programs usually can be had for $5 to $50. Tourist maps with the locations of stars' homes fetch only $1 to $5. Most magazines such as *Photoplay* and *Screen Book* sell for $5 to $20, but covers showing really big stars command more. Spanish magazines featuring Lucille Ball or Raquel Welch sell for nearly $90, and an early *Time* magazine featuring the Marx Brothers recently went for almost $140.

Most movie-star calendars, even ones that feature stars of yesterday, are new and are rarely priced at more than $15 to $20. An exception is the 1955 nude Marilyn Monroe calendar, which sells for $50. However, it's been so widely reproduced that the inexperienced collector would be wise to stay away from it altogether.

Sheet music can be an excellent buy and one that's often overlooked by collectors. Most pieces are priced in the $3-to-$10 range.

Trading-card sets, like calendars, are usually new and sell at just $4 to $6 each. An exception is European tobacco card sets with star likenesses from the 1930s. A complete set of these cards can sell for as much as $175.

Scrapbooks of favorite stars usually bring from $10 to $100. A James Dean scrapbook from the 1950s recently sold for $107, and a vintage Richard Chamberlain book for $305. Paper dolls, pin-back buttons, and other items bearing stars' images may be had for just a few dollars.

The more striking the image and the bigger the star, the higher the price will be. A magazine cover with Marilyn Monroe in a sultry pose will always be worth more than a similar cover with Susan Kohner (a minor star of the late 50s and early 60s). It's best to concentrate on collecting just one or two of your idols to keep your collection manageable.

For beginners, the best place to buy movie ephemera is specialized paper shows, where dealers will give you lots of helpful guidance and where you can examine each piece before buying. But first do your homework on eBay, so you'll have an idea about price and availability. Then you'll know when you're getting a good deal.

To learn more:
- On eBay, go to Books, Movie, Music>Memorabilia>Hollywood, then search by individual item, such as "program" or "scrapbook"
- On eBay, go to Books, Movie, Music>Memorabilia>Movies, then search by individual item
- Search the Internet Movie Database at www.imdb.com

Movie-star photographs from 1916 through the '20s, Jacksonville, Florida, studios. Promotion photos and an album of snapshots document the travels of a group of silent-era movie comedians including Oliver Hardy. *Photo courtesy of Skinner, Inc.*

Are there currently any movie-poster bargains?

Juvenile-delinquent and hot-rod movies from the '50s are still relatively inexpensive, and they have wonderfully lurid graphics and tag lines. The only other posters still available at bargain prices are those from current films. Of course, it will be years before the market decides which of them will become valuable collectibles.

How can I improve on the posters I've already collected?

Two words: Trade up. If you know that a poster you want turns up fairly often, hold out for the best example you can find. But if it's a rarity you're after, it may show up only once in your lifetime. Grab it while you can, in whatever condition it's in, and hope to trade up to a better example later. Remember—most collectors simply don't have the money to buy everything they "sort of" want—only what they *really* want.

What records should I keep?

It's important to maintain accurate and up-to-date records to document and protect the value of your collection.

- **Receipts.** Whenever possible, retain the original dated receipt for each item you acquire. This is especially important if you're able to deduct any of your purchases for tax purposes.

- **Dealer contacts.** You may need to contact the dealer later because of a problem with a piece, or you may want to sell back or trade up with him, or have him watch out for a particular item for you.

- **A collection inventory.** Whether you go with a handwritten notebook or opt to use a dedicated software program for collectibles, you'll want to note the date each item was purchased; the name, address, phone number, and e-mail address and Web site of the seller; a description of the item, including its size, age, and condition (including any repairs or restoration); and the purchase price, noting any discount you received from the original asking price. If the seller made any guarantees or representations concerning the item, note these too.

- **Photos and videotapes.** Photos and videos let you record details about your collection that you may never think to make note of, and they could be key to filing an insurance claim in the event of loss. With digital technology, it's now easy to store your photos on the hard drive of your computer and send them over the Internet to other dealers and collectors.

Keeping good records is one thing; protecting them is another. Be sure to keep a backup copy of your inventory and to store it along with receipts and photographic records in a safe place separate from your collection, such as a bank safe-deposit box.

Do I need to have my collection appraised?

An appraisal is an estimate of the value of an object by an expert in the field. It should completely describe the item, noting its age, dimensions, rarity, condition, and approximate value. If you have an extensive and expensive poster collection, an appraisal is a good idea to ensure that your insurance coverage is adequate. If you've assembled your collection over a long time, you may be out of touch with current prices. And if you ever decide to donate items to a charity or institution for a tax benefit, you'll need an appraisal to claim your deduction.

Keep in mind, though, that an appraisal is only as good as the expertise of the appraiser. Where the relatively young field of movie paper is concerned, you'll find that most general appraisers aren't very knowledgeable. You may be able to find an accredited specialist appraiser, but if not you may need to work through a general appraiser and have him or her consult a poster specialist— a dealer or advanced collector—to develop an accurate and well-informed appraisal. Don't hesitate to propose this to the appraiser.

Should I carry separate insurance on my collection?

That depends. You need to weigh the cost of the insurance against the value of your collection and the financial impact you'd suffer if you lost it. Some homeowner's policies cover collections. More likely, you'll need a special rider or even a separate policy—possibly from a different company, one which specializes in collectibles. In any case, make sure the policy covers losses from water damage (such as flood or burst pipes) as well as from fire and theft. And consider a policy that automatically provides increased coverage at regular intervals as your collection appreciates in value.

Bally Books and Press Kits

The studios provided publicity booklets variously called press books, exhibitor campaign manuals, and bally (for ballyhoo) books to theater managers to assist them in selling their films to the public. In the beginning they were simple folders, but by the 1930s they'd expanded into multipage, large-format publications. The press books of Metro-Goldwyn-Mayer, the most profitable studio of the '30s, were especially elaborate, many having full-color covers illustrating the variety of posters, ranging in size from the midget window cards (8" x 14") to the huge twenty-four-sheets (9' x 20'), available to the exhibitor from the studio exchange. The style variants of posters produced for a particular film are also identified, usually by letter, making press books an invaluable reference for the range of material available on a favorite movie.

China Seas, 1935, MGM, press book (front cover). Photo courtesy of Michael B. King.

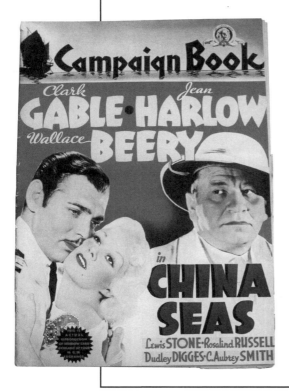

Bally Books

To take a typical example, the press book for *China Seas* (1935), a glossy melodrama from MGM, measures 14" x 20" and boasts a whopping thirty-four pages. Starring Clark Gable, Jean Harlow, and Wallace Beery, the film is a thinly disguised (and sanitized) remake of the studio's steamy megahit *Red Dust,* released just three years earlier. The stars are clearly the selling point in this production.

Divided into three parts—publicity, advertising, and a pullout exploitation (ballyhoo) section—the manual takes the exhibitor step by step through the process of selling the film to the public. The publicity section consists of prepared stories on the stars and background on the film to send to the local press. Portrait and scene stills are illustrated with their identification numbers so they can be ordered from the studio exchange. The advertising section features the newspaper ad campaign in a variety of sizes. Finally, the exploitation section suggests promotional stunts and contests designed to lure the masses into the theater, from cutting out the stars' heads from the twenty-four-sheet poster for a marquee display to sponsoring a contest entitled "Why I Want to Visit the Romantic China Seas."

Even some of the "poverty row" studios had impressive press books, albeit on a smaller scale. For *Pinto Rustlers* (1936), a Tom Tyler B Western, Reliable Pictures produced an eight-page campaign book, 12" wide x 17" high, featuring the latest Art Deco graphics printed in two colors. Not bad for a film that was probably shot in four days! The advertising materials for this mini-epic are impressive, too, including six-, three-, and one-sheet posters, as well as two half-sheets, an insert, and eight lobby cards, all lithographed in full color. In addition, there's a set of twenty-five black-and-white stills and a glass slide using art from one of the half-sheets. Talk about support! How could this picture fail to turn a profit?

Substantial press books continued to be produced into the 1940s, but by the late '50s they were largely printed in black-and-white and were but shadows of their former selves. One studio that proved an exception was Walt Disney, which continued to create elaborate manuals for the reissue of its animated classics, as well as for new films. The press book it used to launch the $20 million deep-space adventure *The Black Hole* (1979) is a throwback to the

China Seas press book (back cover), displaying the poster styles and formats available to theaters. *Photo courtesy of Michael B. King.*

Pinto Rustlers,
1936, Reliable,
press book
(front and back
covers). *Photos
courtesy of
Michael B.
King.*

glory days of ballyhoo, boasting a computer-graphics cover in full color and twenty-four high-tech pages.

As more and more attention (and money) went to promoting pictures on television, studios drastically cut back on their posters and ancillary promotions—in most cases, to a basic one-sheet. This signaled the end of a unique graphic tradition in American popular culture.

Since press books were often literally cut to pieces by theater managers during the run of a film, many were thrown out after use. Of those that have survived more or less intact, the most desirable are from the important films of the '30s and '40s, some of which have made their way to the major auction houses in recent years. As usual, those most in demand are from classic science-fiction, horror, and fantasy films, and condition is a major factor.

The granddaddy of all monster films, featuring the "Eighth Wonder of the World," may be *King Kong* (RKO, 1933). At Sotheby's in 1996, a press book from the film's original release pulled in a gargantuan $4,048. Not far behind is the manual for *Dracula* (Universal, 1931), which brought $3,910 at auction in 1998. A press book for *The Wizard of Oz* (MGM, 1939) fetched a hefty $2,875 in 1996, and one for the original 1937 *Snow White and the Seven Dwarfs* (Disney) brought $345 the same year. Press books with crossover collector appeal can bring substantial prices, as did the 1954 exhibitor campaign book for a series of *Superman* movies starring George Reeves, which recently netted $760.

For collectors whose pockets aren't so deep, press books on such titles as *Affair in Trinidad* (Columbia, 1952), starring Rita Hayworth, may be found for around $60. Newer examples, such as the sixteen-page manual for Woody Allen's *Manhattan* (United Artists, 1979), can be purchased for under $10.

Even though press books from the 1950s and earlier are rare, metropolitan-area memorabilia shops, film conventions, paper shows, and, of course, auction sites are good places to track them down.

Press Kits

Press kits are folders, measuring approximately 9" wide by 12" high, which contain stills and typewritten material created by the studios to publicize films in newspapers and magazines—generally the same materials found in the publicity section of the film's press book.

Press-kit folders are sometimes printed in color, but the stills for films from the '70s and '80s usually are in black-and-white. When the news media began to utilize color, some studios enclosed 35 mm slides in their press kits. Today, press kits are apt to include images on a CD-ROM, such as the kit from Steven Spielberg's *Saving Private Ryan* (DreamWorks, 1998).

The press kit from John Boorman's *The Emerald Forest* (Avco Embassy, 1985) is ½" thick and contains ten black-and-white stills from the film, along with a color program folder, which includes the complete cast and credits. The photographs are quite handsome, but lack the detail and clarity of those from the 1950s and earlier, when cameras for producing 8" x 10" stills were in use.

Press kits for both older and current films can be found in movie-memorabilia shops in major cities, at film conventions and paper shows, and on auction sites such as eBay. They're relatively inexpensive, depending on the number of stills and other components they contain: some may be purchased for under $10.

The Emerald Forest, 1985, Avco Embassy, press kit. John Boorman's mesmerizing meditation on the clash between two cultures, based on an actual 1972 newspaper account, concerns an American's ten-year search for his young son, kidnapped by a band of Indians on the edge of the Amazon rainforest. *Photo courtesy of Michael B. King.*

A Connecticut Yankee, 1931, Fox, window card. Discovered by Florenz Ziegfeld on stage cracking jokes while spinning a lariat, Will Rogers became America's cowboy philosopher, a roving ambassador of Americana and spokesman for common folk everywhere. His film debut was in 1918, but it wasn't until the coming of sound that his gifts were fully realized. *A Connecticut Yankee,* Mark Twain's tale of a man who travels back in time to King Arthur's court, was the perfect vehicle for Rogers's homespun humor and political satire. When Rogers died in a plane crash, four years after making this film, the entire nation mourned. *Photo courtesy of Michael B. King.*

A Connecticut Yankee in King Arthur's Court, 1949, Paramount, one-sheet. Bing Crosby croons his way through Camelot in this later version of the Mark Twain satire. *Photo courtesy of Chisholm-Larsson Gallery.*

LIVING WITH YOUR COLLECTION

Nothing enlivens a space like movie graphics. They make no pretense about being fine art—they're fun, plain and simple. They evoke memories, break the ice, and stimulate conversation. And as you'll soon discover, displaying your movie posters and stills is one of the true joys of this pursuit. It gives you the chance to share your passion (and maybe even kindle it in others).

Protecting, Displaying, and Storing Your Collection

What should I do to protect and preserve my collection?

Rule number one is what you *shouldn't* do: Never dry-mount your paper collectibles or glue them to a hard backing such as foam-core board. The only acceptable mounting is an archival paper-and-linen backing applied by a professional restorer. This is sometimes necessary if the poster came in multiple pieces (such as a three-sheet) or if it's torn.

Half-sheets and inserts were almost always folded by the poster exchanges which distributed them, and because they were printed on heavier cardboard they can have very noticeable folds. Professional mounting on archival paper (also known as Japanese paper) after a deacidifying wash can make a poster that was in deplorable condition look as good as new. Always ask the restorer to add an inch or so of paper around the edges of the poster to protect it from crumpling in storage or transit, and to make matting and framing easier, especially if you want to show the entire poster.

Are there other precautions I should take?

You should avoid exposing your posters, stills, and other paper collectibles to direct sunlight or even bright artificial lighting. Some collectors install draperies, shutters, or blinds to maintain low light levels where prized collectibles are on display. If artificial lighting is used, it should never be aimed directly at the pieces (which will be "cooked" over time) but toward the floor. This not only protects posters and photographs but shows them at their best, in ambient light.

Where should I display my pieces?

Certainly very few rooms are able to accommodate a huge three-sheet poster (41" x 81"), but most can handle a collection of one-sheets (27" x 41"). For smaller spaces (such as foyers, stairs, and hallways), there are half-sheets (22" x 28"), inserts (14" x 36"), and lobby cards (11" x 14").

A media room or home theater is a natural place to put posters and stills on display, perhaps rotating pieces to suit the season (such as Halloween and Christmas). It's a wonderful way to set the mood for viewing a film or throwing a party. And a traditional wood-paneled den or study is tailor-made for a display of the classic cowboy heroes, such as Tom Mix, Buck Jones, and William "Hopalong Cassidy" Boyd. The stone lithographs produced for the Westerns of the '20s and early '30s are incredibly rich in color and really come to life in such a brandy-and-cigars setting.

Are there areas of my home where I shouldn't store or display my collection?

Yes, and they're all the usual suspects. For storage, avoid garages, attics, and basements—areas where fluctuations of temperature and humidity can wreak havoc on delicate paper. And think twice before displaying pieces in areas prone to excessive moisture (such as a bathroom) or airborne grease (such as in or near a kitchen).

Spellbound, 1945, RKO, one-sheet. Hampered by producer David O. Selznik's interference, Alfred Hitchcock called *Spellbound* "just another manhunt story wrapped up in pseudo-psychoanalysis." The film is notable for the famous Salvador Dalí dream sequence and for Ingrid Bergman's radiant performance. This example is well worth restoring with a paper-and-linen backing and fill-in paper on the borders. *Photo courtesy of Chisholm-Larsson Gallery.*

Gone with the Wind

When Clark Cable turned to Vivien Leigh and uttered those words "Frankly, my dear, I don't give a damn!," he launched a cult whose fascination with the 1939 film *Gone with the Wind* (or simply GWTW in buffspeak) hasn't waned since. One of the most popular movies of all time, it has spawned thousands of collectibles, including jewelry and lamps. American manufacturers, realizing that this film would be big, rushed to produce myriad tie-in items. A set of figural Rhett Butler and Scarlett O'Hara bookends produced before the roles were even cast sells today for $2,500.

Typing "Gone with the Wind" into the search box on eBay will usually bring up some two thousand items, ranging from a biography of Margaret Mitchell, author of the original book, to a GWTW board game, with Rhett and Scarlett paper dolls. In fact, dolls are among the most plentiful GWTW collectibles on the market.

A GWTW Barbie set by Mattel, with five dolls, backdrop, and video about Vivien Leigh, sells for about $250. Madame Alexander produced a series of Scarlett dolls, each in a different costume. And Prissy, who knew "nothin' about birthin' babies," has been honored with a 1989 doll made by World that sells for about $250.

Another interesting category of GWTW collectibles is hair accessories; most of the styles actually predated the film and were simply labeled Scarlett O'Hara merchandise. These include hair nets, snoods, and hair bows; all feature "Gone with the Wind" packaging, which is what attracts collectors, and sell in the $1-to-$10 range.

In addition, there are numerous limited-edition plates featuring the images of Rhett, Scarlett, and the rest of the characters. A popular and pricey version is a set of twelve miniature plates with a two-tier wooden "antebellum" display unit that sells for $200.

Whatever your collectible preference, the most desirable element is that southern antebellum flavor. The more a piece makes you want to drawl, the better it is.

As a beginning collector, you should be aware that production of memorabilia from this film continues to this day and that the older items, contemporary with the picture's release in 1939, are by far the most valuable. If you're unsure of an item's vintage, ask lots of questions and get a detailed written receipt. And bear in mind that a "Gone with the Wind lamp" is merely in the style of the movie's set decor and not necessarily an actual item from the film.

eBay offerings in this category are dominated by books, dolls, and plates, so you may want to look elsewhere for some variety. The *Gone with the Wind* Web ring is a great place to start; if you can't find anything to buy here, you'll at least make contact with other enthusiasts who can help you find vintage memorabilia. eMerchandise carries a large inventory of licensed merchandise.

To learn more:

- "Gone with the Wind" Web ring: www.dreamweb.org/gonewiththewindring
- eMerchandise: www.emerchandise.com
- *"Frankly, My Dear . . . ": Gone with the Wind Memorabilia,* Herb Bridges
- *Hollywood Jewels,* Penny Proddow

Gone with the Wind, 1939, MGM, insert. One of the most popular movies of all time (it has been called the first blockbuster), *Gone with the Wind* was nominated for thirteen Academy Awards and won eight statuettes, including for best picture. *Photo courtesy of Michael B. King.*

Framing Your Collection

How should I frame my movie posters?

It may sound strange, but for one-sheets and larger posters, ordinary screen-door molding from your local lumberyard or hardware store works just fine. It comes in 2" to 3" widths, is 1" thick, and already has a nice groove for accepting the screening material. If you'd like something fancier, there are stock moldings with neoclassical or Art Deco elements that you can paint to look like a poster case from a downtown movie palace.

After you've cut the molding and assembled your frame, have a piece of thin acrylic glazing (such as Plexiglas) cut to fit into the groove in your frame by a plastics supplier. Specify UV-screening glazing, to screen out harmful ultraviolet rays, which can cause posters to fade. For a backing, use acid-free foam core, available at art-supply stores. Never use ordinary cardboard; it contains potentially damaging acids and absorbs moisture, which can cause your posters to wrinkle and stain.

What if I'm just not handy with tools?

No problem. If you're not the do-it-yourself type, professional framers have all the necessary materials on hand and will be more than happy to supply the skill. Expect to spend anywhere from $200 to $300 to have a one-sheet poster professionally framed, compared with a materials cost of less than $50 if you do the work yourself.

When you visit a professional frame shop, it's easy to be overwhelmed by the range of frame styles and colors on display. Don't hesitate to ask for the framer's advice (it's what you're paying for, after all), and keep these tips in mind:

- For a color image, consider making the frame one of the colors used in the image.
- Portraits and still photographs often look their best in black or natural wood frames with a simple, wide mat. If the photo has aged to a sepia tone, use an off-white or cream-color mat in a natural-wood frame. If the image has strong blacks, medium grays, and brilliant whites, an antique-white mat and a black frame will add a note of understated elegance. Silver or pewter may also complement the image.

Aren't there standard poster frames I can buy to save money?

Indeed there are. Metal sectional frames come in a range of standard sizes (and in a variety of colors), but generally only for smaller posters, such as half-sheets (22" x 28") and inserts (14" x 36"). Once again, you can pick a color used in the poster for the frame. For example, the *Goldfinger* (United Artists, 1964) half-sheet looks great in a bronze sectional frame. Some collectors prefer to stay with silver or basic black for their entire collection.

For lobby cards, the easiest off-the-shelf solution is 11" x 14" clear acrylic box frames, which you can find at a photography shop or art-supply store. Hanging in groups of four on each side of a framed one-sheet from the same film, they make a stunning display that evokes memories of the great movie houses of days gone by.

Are there any special precautions I should take in framing?

Especially for still photographs, use only a UV-screening acrylic glazing, such as Plexiglas (available from a plastics supplier or at art-supply stores). The silver-halide crystals in photo emulsions are even more sensitive to light than the lithographic inks used in posters. Attach photographs to acid-free mounting boards with acid-free corners, both of which are available at photography shops. For both stills and posters, use an acid-free mat to set off the image and keep it from coming in contact with the glazing.

What if a poster needs a minor repair before it's framed?

It's always best to use the services of a professional restorer for poster repairs. But if that's not possible or practical, and the repair is essential to save the poster (to avoid losing a torn corner, for example), you may decide to undertake it yourself. Use only an acid-free document-repair tape—such as Filmoplast P—which is available at stores for office, library, and art supplies, as well as from online sources such as www.snco.com and www.kapco.com. Under no circumstances should you use ordinary masking tape, which dries, turns crusty, and stains.

Resources for Living with Your Collection

Graphik Dimensions Ltd.
2103 Brentwood Street
High Point, NC 27263
Telephone: 336-887-3700
Web site: www.pictureframes.com
Metal sectional frames in many colors, several styles, and sizes up to 48". Ready-made frames for photos in standard sizes and several colors, complete with acid-free wide presentation mat, clear acrylic glazing, and backing board.

Light Impressions
P.O. Box 22708
Rochester, NY 14692-2708
Telephone: 800-826-6216
Web site: www.lightimpressionsdirect.com
Acid-free mending tapes, mounting corners, storage boxes, and mat board; Plexiglas, frames, and more.

Talas
568 Broadway
New York, NY 10012
Telephone: 212-219-0770
Web site: www.talas-nyc.com
A full-line supplier of conservation, preservation, and restoration supplies.

The Seven Year Itch, 1955, Twentieth Century Fox, half-sheet. The iconic image of Monroe standing on a subway grate, her white dress billowing up around her, was shot on Manhattan's Lexington Avenue at 52nd Street. Billy Wilder didn't use the footage in the film, however; he restaged the scene in the studio. *Photo courtesy of Michael B. King.*

Movie Stills

The 8" x 10" black-and-white glossy photo has been a staple of the film industry since its humble beginnings. Produced in huge quantities from the 1920s through the 1950s, the best of them are forever etched in our minds like old friends: King Kong atop the Empire State Building, Charles Foster Kane against the backdrop of his giant portrait, Marilyn Monroe standing on a subway grating with her white dress billowing around her. These images are so compelling that they've come to represent the films themselves, even though they were specially made for publicity purposes. In fact, the scenes they're meant to be taken from may be presented quite differently on-screen, or may not appear in the film at all.

A "still" refers to a photograph of actors or scenes from a film or production of a film made for publicity or documentary purposes. Staged scenes, portraits of stars or supporting players, and action and production shots all qualify as stills. Action stills are actually taken during filming and depict stunt work and/or elaborate effects. Production stills depict the filmmaking process itself, often with the lights and cameras in view. They can convey the sense of magic and mystery inherent in the act of creation. There are also costume-test stills and stills of sets devoid of actors, made for continuity purposes.

Stills of all kinds were sent in large numbers to theater managers, magazines, and newspapers. Theater managers could visit the studio exchanges (and later the National Screen Service) and select images, either to be displayed in the lobby or blown up for elaborate marquee displays.

Portrait stills have become the subject of several large-format coffee-table books in recent years, propelling them to the forefront of movie collectibles. They've appeared in feature articles in glossy magazines such as *Architectural Digest* as decor accessories. It's no wonder, when portrait stills such as those made of Greta Garbo for *Mata Hari* (MGM, 1931) by Clarence Sinclair Bull, head of the stills department at the studio at the time (and her favorite photographer), are works of art.

In the 1920s, Metro-Goldwyn-Mayer was the first studio to create its own in-house stills department rather than hire outside photographers. From 1925 to 1929, the department was headed by Ruth Harriet Louise, the only woman among the top photographers in Hollywood. Her portraits are sensuous and soft, bringing out the feminine side of Garbo, Crawford, Norma Shearer, Marion Davies, and the other Metro ladies. Because she retired at the peak of her career to get married, her portraits are extremely rare and highly coveted.

With "More stars than there are in heaven" as its motto, MGM became the most successful studio in Hollywood during the 1930s. During this period, legendary photographer George Hurrell worked at MGM, where Joan Crawford was his favorite subject. Crawford, unlike many of her contemporaries, actually enjoyed being photographed and worked tirelessly to make their sessions productive. The body of work they produced during their years at the studio is extraordinary in its originality, with Crawford seeming to reinvent herself anew for each session.

In addition to the standard 8" x 10" photos, special 11" x 14" portrait stills and production shots were sent to fan magazines and major market newspapers. They were produced in this larger size, sometimes in sepia tone, to afford superb reproduction when printed in the rotogravure sections of these publications. Needless to say, they're much sought after by collectors.

Is it any wonder that some studio employees, theater ushers, projectionists, and fan-magazine

Greta Garbo, ca. 1929, portrait still by Clarence Sinclair Bull for MGM. Perhaps the dean of Hollywood photographers, Bull became the enigmatic Swedish star's exclusive photographer after Ruth Harriet Louise left the studio in 1930. Known as "the man who shot Garbo," Bull amassed more than two thousand negatives of her during their collaboration from 1929 to 1941; this stunning portrait is believed to be from one of their earliest sessions together. *Photo courtesy of Michael B. King.*

and newspaper editors saved the stills and portraits that came their way? A good thing, too, since many films from the silent era have been lost. The only records we have of Lon Chaney's legendary *London after Midnight* (MGM, 1927), for example, are the photographs taken during production. Now even the 8" x 10" nitrate negatives are beginning to deteriorate, and some no longer yield a satisfactory image.

Because still photographers from the earliest days through the 1950s typically used a large-format camera, which produced an 8" x 10" negative, their images are incredibly clear. Many details, such as the weave in the fabrics of costumes, a microphone boom, or the texture of a painted backdrop, are visible in stills whereas they are undetectable when one views the film.

One of the pleasures in collecting stills is that they were produced in such numbers that one can always find something new on a favorite star or film. Another plus is their affordability. They're nowhere near as expensive as posters and lobby cards. In the New York and Los Angeles memorabilia shops, one can expect to pay from $3.50 to $5 for a reprint from an original negative. Vintage stills from the original year of release, if they're available on older titles, command $10 and up. There are even "dollar boxes" at film conventions where one can find unexpected gems.

One can expect to pay considerably more ($1,000 and up) for vintage portraits of such major stars as Garbo, Crawford, Clara Bow (usually photographed by Paramount's Eugene Robert Richee), Marilyn Monroe, and Grace Kelly, especially if they have the photographer's stamp embossed in the front margin or on the back. As for genre, original stills from the Universal horror films of the early 1930s command the highest prices, as do stills from the classic German Expressionist works, such as *The Cabinet of Dr. Caligari* (Decla-Bioskop, 1916) and *Metropolis* (UFA/Paramount, 1926).

As with any paper collectible, condition is key in determining price. A vintage still is apt to have pinholes or tape on its corners. The more popular the film, the more likely that the photograph saw extensive use. Some stills were trimmed. Others may have notes scribbled on the back. All of these defects can detract from the desirability of the piece.

Studio stills can be found in movie-memorabilia shops in New York City, Los Angeles, and other metropolitan areas; paper-ephemera shows; antiques shops; the Cinefest show in Syracuse, New York; from fellow collectors; and on eBay and other online auctions. Collectors need to be wary of duplicates, which have been made from some of the most popular stills (on occasion, the dupes themselves have been copied; the quality of the image becomes progressively worse with each generation away from the original print). With today's digital technology it's sometimes difficult to spot a copy, but here are some tips.

An original gelatin silver print still has a full range of values—from black to gray to white. There is no loss of detail, even in the deepest blacks or the highest lights. Moreover, vintage prints from the 1920s through the 1950s possess a shimmering, silvery quality, and sometimes a warm tone, which come from varying densities of silver-halide crystals on the surface of the paper.

In the case of 8" x 10" contact prints, the focus is incredibly clear (although some photographers, especially during the 1920s, opted for a soft-focus effect in portraits; in extreme cases, the eye of the subject that's closest to the camera may be the only area in sharp focus). Another way to spot an original is to look carefully at the identification numbers at the bottom: they should be the brilliant white of the paper, because they were hand-printed on the negative in black ink.

The paper used in the '20s lends exceptional depth and luminosity to images. The back has a textured, papery feel; if one lightly marks on the back border area with a pencil, it leaves a mark. In the 1950s, paper began to be coated with resin to shorten the fixing and drying time. Resin-coated paper yields an image that lacks the glow of non-coated stock. It has a plastic or rubbery feel. If one takes a pencil to it, it slips and barely leaves a mark.

Original stills may or may not have the film's title and studio printed in the bottom margin. Most '20s and some '30s originals lack this data. MGM mimeographed this information on the backs of its photographs.

Production still from *The Bride Word Red,* 1937, MGM. *Photo courtesy of Michael B. King.*

Every studio had its own system for identifying stills, usually by marking in one of the lower corners of the image. When you're going through a box of stills at a paper show, knowing something about these systems will help you identify the studio and perhaps the title. In the case of a production shot from MGM's *The Bride Wore Red* (1937) depicting Joan Crawford and George Zucco under the watchful eye of Dorothy Arzner, one of Hollywood's first women directors, the number 997 indicates the film, the letter X identifies the photographer (Clarence Sinclair Bull), and the number 111 specifies the individual still. Warner Bros. used key letters from the film's title. In a *Charge of the Light Brigade* (Warner Bros., 1936) photo depicting Errol Flynn on horseback in the heat of battle, we see the letters LB followed by the still number, 542, and A (for "action"). In the mid-1940s, the studio switched to a number system for the film's title. Universal also used

Action still from *The Charge of the Light Brigade,* 1936, Warner Bros. Breathtaking though the final charge may be, with Errol Flynn clearly doing his own riding, it's also disturbing if you know that several horses were killed during its filming. The resulting furor, which included a lawsuit brought by animal-rights activists, forced moviemakers to devise safer stunts. *Photo courtesy of Michael B. King.*

a number system, as seen on a still from *The Old Dark House* (1932): 542 identifies the title, and 1-31 represents the still number. Paramount also used numbers, and Fox placed numbers in the upper right margin.

RKO used a letter system for the title, then the still number. *Bird of Paradise* (1932) is BP, *Swing Time* (1936) is NG (for *Never Gonna Dance,* the film's original title), and *Out of the Past* (1947) is BG (for *Build My Gallows High,* another discarded title).

In the 1950s, MGM and some other studios began to issue color stills for their color releases, some of which were lithographed in England, producing a Technicolor effect. Some examples include a wonderful shot of Vittorio De Sica, Edward G. Robinson, and Raquel Welch riding in a Venetian gondola from *The Biggest Bundle of Them All* (MGM, 1967), and a shot from Stanley Kubrick's *2001: A Space Odyssey* (MGM, 1968). By the mid-1960s, virtually all Hollywood movies were filmed in color, bringing to an end the glorious era of black-and-white cinematography.

For storage and display, photographs should never be taped or glued to a backing. Any necessary repairs should be made on the back of the print with acid-free tape. For framing, always use acid-free materials: clear archival mounting corners on mat board, then a mat to keep the print from touching the glass or UV-screening Plexiglas. Finally, be sure to display your treasures away from direct sunlight.

As François Truffaut, the French director, once said, "If a film has one good shot, it's worth sitting through the entire picture just to see it." Well, that may be a bit of an exaggeration—especially when we have the stills to enjoy. Happy hunting!

Still from *The Old Dark House,* 1932, Universal. This trapped-in-a-spooky-house classic was directed by James Whale, who would later be portrayed by Ian McKellan in the critically acclaimed *Gods and Monsters*. Gloria Stuart, who scored an Academy Award–nominated comeback in *Titanic* in 1997, is shown with the menacing Boris Karloff. *Photo courtesy of Michael B. King.*

"OLD DARK HOUSE" A UNIVERSAL PRODUCTION

You Only Live Twice, 1967, United Artists, insert. The fifth James Bond film has Sean Connery's debonair British agent in a deadly race to prevent nuclear war at the hands of SPECTRE's Blofeld (Donald Pleasence). Bond fakes his death to go under cover to find the villain's launching station, located inside a Japanese volcano—one of the most spectacular settings in any 007 production. The graphics of this insert convey the giddy atmosphere of the film.
Photo courtesy of Michael B. King.

IF AND WHEN YOU DECIDE TO SELL

Why You Might Want to
Sell All or Part of Your Collection

As great as your passion for movie posters and memorabilia may be, at some point you may want or need to sell some or all of your collection. When you do, you'll find that there are a variety of ways to go about it—some quicker than others, some more work than others, and some more likely than others to turn you a profit.

Personal circumstances change. Perhaps your collecting budget is greater now than it was when you first started; today, scarcer and more desirable posters are your game, and the more common ones you bought a few years ago no longer hold as much appeal. Perhaps you're contemplating financing a major purchase or expense—a new home or a college education—and the money you've invested in your collection needs to be freed up (if only for a time). Maybe you're downsizing your household, and you simply won't have the space you once enjoyed for your huge collection. Maybe your collection has just gotten too big to enjoy.

Whatever your reason for selling, here's where good record keeping really pays off. If you have every item in your collection described in a database or on a set of inventory forms, it will be easy to review what you have to sell. Being able to look up what you paid for items will help you set your prices. If you took care to capture the details of an item's condition and history, you've already gone a long way toward writing a listing—whether for an ad, a price tag, or an online auction.

You Want to Trade Up or Your Interest Has Changed

One of the most common reasons to sell is to trade up. Perhaps you've found an example in much better condition than the item you already own. Maybe you've zeroed in on your collecting specialty, and some of your pieces are outside the scope of that theme.

What do you do with pieces you've outgrown? The next time you go to a collectibles show, try taking a couple of your extra pieces along, and see if you can find a dealer who will buy them or trade with you. It's largely a hit-or-miss proposition, but the worst-case scenario is that you'll have to take the pieces back home at the end of the day. If you have a rare item, it's probably best to sell it rather than trade it.

You Need the Money

Selling your collection because you need the money is never an ideal situation, but let's face it: kids need braces and college tuition has to be paid. Urgent situations like an illness, a job loss, or a move also may force you to sell. Again, if you've kept good records, you should be able to liquidate fairly quickly and find several different sales avenues to explore.

Ways to Sell

Sell the Entire Collection to a Dealer

This option will probably net you the lowest return on the money you've invested, since dealers typically pay only a percentage of current market value—usually 50 percent or less. But if you've held your pieces for a long time, even the wholesale prices a dealer will pay could net you a gain over what you originally paid. Or you may be lucky enough to own items that have become much more desirable since you bought them.

If you live near a major metropolitan area, you may be better served visiting dealers there as opposed to in your local market. Demand for movie memorabilia is higher in metropolitan markets, and dealers there generally will pay you a higher price as a result.

Depending on your circumstances, the speed, ease, and convenience of selling your collection as a whole may outweigh the money issue. You'll avoid many of the headaches of selling, such as keeping track of individual sales and packing and shipping your items—not to mention bad checks, disgruntled purchasers, and being stuck with items that just won't move.

Consign Your Collection to a Dealer

You may get more money for your collection by consigning it to a dealer, but it will take longer to sell it. Here, you definitely need to have an item-by-item inventory and establish a specific price for each piece. You may also need to discuss your price expectations with the consignee. Although the dealer is going to get a percentage of the selling price as his commission, he'll be reluctant to handle an item if you have unrealistic price expectations that may keep it in his inventory for too long. Clarify the details of your arrangement and get them in writing, signed by both of you.

One of the best reasons to enter into an arrangement like this is that full-time dealers cover more ground than you do—operating at shows, in their shops, and even on the Internet simultaneously. They also have many more contacts than you have, and a supply of want lists from other collectors who are ready to buy. The commission you pay to get access to a dealer's selling network is well worth it.

Sell Your Collection Yourself

This is the most time-consuming way to sell a collection, both in terms of what you'll have to put into it as well as how long it may take to sell. Not only will you need to be on top of the market, you'll also have to present your items for sale, establish a network of contacts as you look for potential customers, and (if you're selling by mail or online) follow through on every transaction.

The Navigator, 1924, Metro-Goldwyn, window card. Rivaled only by Charlie Chaplin in his mastery of screen comedy, Buster Keaton produced ten features between 1923 and 1928. In the most commercially successful of them, *The Navigator,* Keaton generates innumerable wildly incredible comic situations from a single prop, a deserted ocean liner, and faces them with a fundamental calm that is the essence of his appeal. *Photo courtesy of Michael B. King.*

You'll be on the other side of customer-service hassles such as bad checks, complaints, tracking shipments—the whole deal. If you run an ad in a collectors' magazine or trade paper, you'll have to put up money with no guarantee that you'll ever make it back. Also, the lead time for placing such ads can absorb precious weeks before anyone even sees it.

The Internet is the most popular venue for a self-seller, but it has its drawbacks. If you use one of the big online auctions such as eBay, Amazon, or Yahoo and you make an innocent mistake or fail to hold up your end of a transaction, it might lead to a posting of negative feedback that will make other buyers wary of you. On the plus side, you're putting your offerings before a wide audience—wider than any individual dealer could deliver. And if you have rarities or highly desirable items to auction, it takes only two people desperate to add a particular piece to their collections to drive the bidding higher than what you could hope to realize from other sources.

Cat on a Hot Tin Roof, 1958, MGM, three-sheet. Production codes dictated that Tennessee Williams's Pulitzer Prize–winning play be "edited" for the screen, but the result is still highly charged. *Photo courtesy of Skinner, Inc.*

Online auctions. An honest, compelling description—complete with good-quality photographs—is essential to a successful sale in an Internet auction. Interested buyers scan a great many ads and click through long lists of page views quickly. If your description doesn't catch their eye, or if it leaves them with obvious questions unanswered, they're likely to move on. Consider the following examples.

A poorly written description:

North by Northwest Super Still

Here is a photo from the classic movie *North by Northwest,* directed by Alfred Hitchcock. It shows Cary Grant standing with two men with guns drawn. It is in excellent condition. Buyer pays $5.00 shipping. International postage higher.

A well-written description:

North by Northwest Super Vintage 1959 Still

Here is an original-release vintage 8 x 10 B&W still from the classic 1959 suspense production *North by Northwest,* starring Cary Grant, Eva Marie Saint, James Mason, and Martin Landau. Directed by the master of suspense, Alfred Hitchcock. In this scene, advertising executive Roger Thornhill (Grant) is "requested at gunpoint" by two unknown assassins (Adam Williams and Roger Ellenstein) to make a radical change in his evening plans, or else . . . Excellent condition. Buyer pays $5.00 shipping. International postage higher.

109

This description provides essential information the potential buyer needs. It's obviously written by a seller who knows his movies and his material. It also features a scan of the photograph, including the identification line at the bottom, which cites the film title, studio, year of release, and copyright information.

Before you start posting items for sale on the Internet, it's a good idea to do some online research. Search completed auctions for comparable items to see how they're described and the kinds of prices they're fetching.

Live auctions. This avenue is quite different from online auctions in that you're putting your pieces in the hands of a professional auctioneer. Your concerns with live auctions should be:

- **Is the auctioneer reputable?** He or she should be a member of a recognized auctioneers' association.
- **Where does the auctioneer advertise, and how effectively?** The results of a live auction depend entirely on the turnout of bidders.
- **Does the auctioneer publish a catalog?** High-end auctions are generally cataloged. Auctioneers who produce catalogs likely have extensive mailing lists to solicit interested collectors.
- **How will the items be sold?** Depending on what you have to sell, you may want the most desirable pieces to be sold individually, with the more common ones grouped in lots.
- **What's the commission?** Auctioneers usually charge a percentage of the amount of the winning bid. If you have a large collection to auction, you may be able to negotiate the commission. It never hurts to ask.

Advertising and mail-order selling. You may want to try placing ads in collectors' magazines or collectibles trade papers. If so, your description will be all-important, as this is generally a two-step selling process. Here's how it works: If your ads are well written, they'll generate correspondence from people who want to know more. When that happens, you've got to be ready to send a more detailed description and photo (a digital image if you're using the Internet) of the items. You may hear back from some of them a second time with more questions or, if you're lucky, start preliminary negotiations on a purchase.

A word to the wise: It's a good idea to protect your privacy by listing only your name, a post-office-box address, phone number, and e-mail address in your ads.

If you're simply selling items from your collection as a sideline, mail order can be a pretty distracting way to do business. You'll get phone calls and voice-mail messages at all times of the day and night, and you'll end up playing a lot of phone tag with callbacks. You've got a lot of work to do, both on the phone and at the post office, to get information to people and answer their questions. That's why most successful mail-order dealers advertise repeatedly and set themselves up to make this a primary sales avenue.

Tarzan and His Mate, 1934, MGM, lobby card. The second of six Johnny Weissmuller and Maureen O'Sullivan jungle adventures, *Tarzan and His Mate* is generally regarded as the most entertaining. *Photo courtesy of Michael B. King.*

The Wizard of Oz

The Wizard of Oz, a film classic first released in 1939, has generated an entire industry in theatrical rereleases, videos (including collectors' and anniversary editions), DVDs, and thousands of related collectibles.

The earliest items, the ones produced close to the 1939 release of the film, are the costliest. On eBay recently, a Gallaher *Wizard of Oz* Judy Garland tobacco card sold

for $38; a *Wizard of Oz* drinking glass for $36; the sheet music to "Over the Rainbow," $102; and a 1939 MGM *Wizard of Oz* sheet of letterhead with envelope, $121. Early licensed merchandise, which was very limited in scope, included Ideal Toys' "Judy Garland as Dorothy" doll and "The Strawman by Ray Bolger" doll. The 18" Judy Garland doll sells today in the $700 range.

The film's memorabilia was produced steadily in many countries in the '40s, '50s, and '60s. But it was the proliferation of items in the 1970s, sparked by the success of the Broadway musical *The Wiz,* numerous television broadcasts of the film (hosted by the likes of Gregory Peck), and a two-season Saturday-Sunday matinee theatrical rerelease of the film, that brought Oz collectibles to the general public. They were less rare and, therefore, less expensive.

The Wizard of Oz, 1949 rerelease, MGM, one-sheet. A poster promoting one of the many rereleases of this enduringly popular film. Judy Garland has clearly aged since her original trip down the Yellow Brick Road, as evidenced by the head shot at the top of the poster. *Photo courtesy of Chisholm-Larsson Gallery.*

Among the best-known Oz collectibles is the series of dolls issued by Mego in 1974. There was a doll for each of the major characters, the most popular of which are Dorothy, the Tinman, the Cowardly Lion, and the Scarecrow. These currently sell for up to $100 each, mint in the box. The Ken and Barbie *Wizard of Oz* set, with five dolls representing the major characters, all in original boxes, sells for up to $400. And pewter replicas of the ruby slippers may be had for $25. Warner Bros. also produced children's versions of the ruby slippers in 1997, and these sell for about $20. If you feel you must have a pair of the 6B slippers actually worn by Judy Garland in the film (four pairs are known to exist), be prepared to spend in the neighborhood of $666,000, the auction price realized by Christie's East in the spring of 2000. One of the Cowardly Lion's pawlike shoes went for nearly $26,000 in the same auction.

Among today's most popular *Wizard of Oz* collectibles are limited-edition plates and holiday ornaments. A Knowles fortieth-anniversary plate from 1979, entitled "The Grand Finale," recently netted $40 on eBay, and a 1995 Enesco 3D Wizard of Oz plate brought $21. A set of twelve Kurt Adler Christmas ball ornaments depicting characters and scenes from the film consistently sells for around $35. In 1989, in celebration of the fiftieth anniversary of the movie, designer Wendy Gell produced a line of figural jewelry featuring its characters. It sold out completely. If you're lucky enough to find a Dorothy brooch from that collection, expect to pay up to $1,000 to acquire it.

For modern Oz collectibles, Warner Bros. stores offer a great selection. Specialized doll-and-toy antiques shows will usually yield older and rarer finds. Typing in "Wizard of Oz" on eBay's search engine will turn up hundreds of items (or you can link through the "Categories" on the front page to get to the complete *Wizard of Oz* listings). Shop around. Most of these items were produced in great numbers, and prices vary.

To learn more:
- *100 Years of Oz,* John Fricke
- *The Wizardry of Oz,* Jay Scarfone and William Stillman
- *The Wizard of Oz: The Official 50th Anniversary Pictorial History,* John Fricke, Jay Scarfone, and William Stillman
- *The Wizard of Oz Collector's Treasury,* Jay Scarfone and William Stillman
- *The Judy Garland Collector's Guide,* Edward R. Pardella
- *Hake's Price Guide to Character Toy Premiums,* Ted Hake
- Jim's Wizard of Oz Web site: www.geocities.com/Hollywood/Hills/6396

RESOURCES TO FURTHER YOUR COLLECTING

Shows

Cinefest
Phil Serling
The Syracuse Cinefile Society
215 Dawley Road
Fayetteville, NY 13066-2546
Telephone: 315-637-8985
Web site: www.picking.com
Comments: This four-day annual convention in Syracuse, New York, now in its twenty-first year, is usually held during the second week in March.

Cinevent
P.O. Box 13463
Columbus, OH 43213
Telephone: 614-229-3555
E-mail: shayes@ee.net
Web site: www.cinevent.com
Comments: This show, with its thirty-year history, is held annually over Memorial Day weekend in Columbus, Ohio.

Hollywood Collectors Show, Inc.
Ray Courts and Sharon Courts
P.O. Box 5040
Spring Hill, FL 34611
Telephone: 352-683-5110
E-mail: hcs@atlantic.net
Web site:
     www.hollywoodcollectorshow.com
Comments: One of the biggest and most popular shows, usually attracting more than one hundred celebrities, held in North Hollywood, San Francisco, and Chicago.

Paper Collectables and Movie Memorabilia Shows
N. Gallagher
417 Hoyt Street
Darien, CT 06820
Telephone: 203-329-1516
Comments: Monthly show held in New York City, with one large weekend show in summer.

Specialist Dealers

Chisholm-Larsson Gallery
145 Eighth Avenue
New York, NY 10011
Telephone: 212-741-1703
Web site:
    www.chisholm-poster.com
Comments: Sells vintage posters.

Cinemonde
138 Second Avenue North,
    Suite 104
Nashville, TN 37201
Telephone: 615-742-3048
Fax: 615-742-1268
E-mail: cinemonde@earthlink.net
Web site: www.cinemonde.com
Comments: Sells vintage posters.

Todd Feiertag
Poster City
P.O. Box 94
Orangeburg, NY 10962
Telephone: 800-272-3323 *or*
    201-869-1692
E-mail: toddfeiertag@msn.com
eBay seller name:
    toddfeiertag@msn.com
Comments: Sells vintage posters
    and lobby cards by mail and
    over the Internet. Also does
    appraisals.

The Last Moving Picture Company
Morris Everett Jr., Owner
10535 Chillicothe Road
Kirtland, OH 44094
Telephone: 440-256-3660
Fax: 440-256-3431
E-mail: lastmo@aol.com
Web site:
    www.vintagefilmposters.com
Comments: Sells vintage posters
    and stills from stores in
    Hollywood, California, and
    Washington, D.C. Also sells
    by mail and over the Internet.

Motion Picture Arts Gallery
133 East 58th Street, Tenth Floor
New York, NY 10022
Telephone: 212-223-1009
Fax: 212-371-0809
Web site: www.mpagallery.com
Comments: Sells vintage posters in
    a gallery setting.

MovieArt Original Film Posters
P.O. Box 4419
Austin, TX 78765
Telephone: 512-479-6680
Fax: 512-480-8225
E-mail: kirby@movieart.net
Web site: www.movieart.net
Comments: Sells original movie
    posters by mail and over the
    Internet.

Movie Star News
134 West 18th Street
New York, NY 10011
Telephone: 212-620-8160
Web site: www.moviestarnews.com
Comments: Sells vintage and
current stills.

**Jerry Ohlinger's Movie
Material Store**
242 West 14th Street
New York, NY 10011
Telephone: 212-989-0869
E-mail: JOMMS@aol.com
Web site: www.moviematerials.com
Comments: Sells vintage and
current stills and posters.

Stephen Sally
339 West 44th Street
New York, NY 10036
Telephone: 212-246-4972
Fax: 201-288-2157
E-mail: Sallypix@aol.com
Comments: Sells vintage
posters and stills (at shows and
by appointment only).

Thornhill Entertainment
Robert M. Cline
P.O. Box 577
Woodleaf, NC 27054
Telephone: 704-636-1116
E-mail: thornhill@cbi1.net
eBay seller name:
thornhillentertainment
Comments: Sells vintage stills and
16 mm films; also sells on eBay.

Auction Houses and Auctions

Christie's East
219 East 67th Street
New York, NY 10021
Telephone: 212-606-0430
Fax: 212-452-2063
Web site: www.christies.com

Sotheby's
1334 York Avenue
New York, NY 10021
Telephone: 212-606-7910
Fax: 212-606-7937
Web site: www.sothebys.com

Vintage Poster Art Auctions
Morris Everett Jr., Director
10535 Chillicothe Road
Kirtland, OH 44094
Telephone: 440-256-3660
Fax: 440-256-3431
E-mail: lastmo@aol.com
Web site:
www.vintagefilmposters.com

Trade Papers, Books, and Magazines

Autograph Collector
Odyssey Publications
510-A South Corona Mall
Corona, CA 91719-1420
Telephone: 909-371-7137
Fax: 909-371-7139
Web site: www.autographs.com

Big Reel

P.O. Box 1050
Dubuque, IA 52004-1050
Telephone: 800-334-7165
Fax: 800-531-0880
Web site: www.collect.com/bigreel
Comments: A monthly
    publication that includes ads,
    show information, and
    convention listings.

Classic Images and
Films of the Golden Age

301 East Third Street
Muscatine, IA 52761
Telephone: 800-383-3198 *or*
    319-263-2331
Fax: 319-262-8042
E-mail: classicimages@
    classicimages.com
Web site: www.classicimages.com
Comments: *Classic Images* is a
    monthly publication with
    articles, ads, and show and
    convention listings. *Films of
    the Golden Age* is a quarterly
    concentrating on film history.

Movie Collector's World

P.O. Box 309
Fraser, MI 48026
Telephone: 810-774-4311
Fax: 810-774-5450
E-mail: mcw@mcwonline.com
Web site: www.mcwonline.com
Comments: Published twice a
    month with ads from dealers
    and collectors, articles, and
    show and convention listings.

Poster Price Almanac

John Kisch, editor
Separate Cinema Publications
P.O. Box 114
Hyde Park, NY 12538
Telephone: 845-452-1998
Fax: 845-454-7131
E-mail: info@posterprice.com
Web site: www.posterprice.com
Comments: A hefty five-hundred-
    plus pages of indispensable
    information on movie-poster
    values, with a huge listing of
    dealers in movie memorabilia.
    Subscription to the Web site
    allows access to up-to-the-
    minute values in Kisch's
    database.

Online Auction Sites
and Databases

eBay.com

Comments: Currently the
    dominant online auction site;
    there are more than a million
    items up for sale at any given
    time. eBay's site is beautifully
    organized, with headings for
    posters, lobby cards, press
    books, photographs, and so
    forth. Go to the heading of
    interest, and type in the
    personality or title you're
    seeking. Because movie glass
    slides are relatively scarce,
    they don't warrant a special
    category. To locate them, go to
    the movie-collectibles search,
    and type in "glass slide."

The Internet Movie Database
www.imdb.com
Comments: This site lists the year,
cast, production credits, and a
synopsis of virtually every film
ever made, including two-reel
silents, comedies, and serials.
They're all here!

Appraisers

**The International Society
of Appraisers**
Telephone: 888-472-5587
Web site: www.isa-appraisers.org

**The American Society
of Appraisers**
Telephone: 800-ASA-VALU *or*
703-478-2228
Web site: www.appraisers.org

**The Appraisers Association
of America**
Telephone: 212-889-5404
Web site: www.appraisersassoc.org

Association of Online Appraisers
Telephone: 301-228-2279
Web site: www.aoaonline.org

Eppraisals.com
Telephone: 877-469-2264
Web site: www.eppraisals.com

Museums and Libraries
**Academy of Motion Picture Arts
and Sciences**
Margaret Herrick Library
333 South La Cienega Boulevard
Beverly Hills, CA 90211
Telephone: 310-247-3000
Web site: www.oscars.org
Comments: Collectors, scholars,
and film buffs may visit the
library during business hours
and see folders of film stills
from the silent era to the
present. Duplicate stills may
also be purchased.

**Museum of Modern Art
(MOMA)**
Department of Film and Video
11 West 53rd Street
New York, NY 10019
Telephone: 212-708-9830
Web site: www.moma.org
Comments: To view MOMA's vast
collection of movie stills, from
the silent era to the present,
make an appointment with
Mary Corliss, curator of film
stills archive. Duplicate stills
may be purchased. The film
and video departments are
being relocated as part of the
museum's expansion; call
ahead for current information.

REPRESENTATIVE VALUE GUIDE

This sampling of movie posters and their values should give the newcomer a sense of the range and price of material in the marketplace. Remember that the combination of a great film, movie-star power, and outstanding graphics is what gives a poster extraordinary value. For this reason, in some cases below we've noted the stars' names in addition to the titles.

For our purposes, assume that the images are complete, with only light usage wear—tack holes, border crumples and minor tears, original fold lines, and theater imprints on those cards and posters that provided spaces for them. The images should present no unusual damage—such as stains, large tears, image areas missing, rodent or insect damage, or excessive fading. Posters sold in the range of prices listed may or may not be paper- or linen-backed.

For those images originally issued in sets (such as lobby cards) the values listed are for a single card (indeed, cards generally bring higher prices when sold individually than when offered as part of a complete set).

Movies with large promotional campaigns often featured more than one style of poster in the popular sizes (we've included here only one example of a style variant, a one-sheet for *The Rocky Horror Picture Show*). Style variants are definitively identified by the studio's original press book, and *Poster Price Almanac*, edited by John Kisch, provides guidance on differences in value among them.

Film	Year	Studio	Value
Midget window card (8" x 14", vertical)			
Broadway Bill	1934	Columbia	$200–$250
King of Chinatown	1939	Paramount	$150–$175
Maryland	1940	Twentieth Century Fox	$40–$50
Stowaway (Shirley Temple)	1936	Twentieth Century Fox	$200–$250
Lobby card (11" x 14", horizontal)			
High Society	1956	MGM	$65–$80
I'm No Angel (Mae West)	1933	Paramount	$400–$500
Invasion of the Body Snatchers	1956	Allied Artists	$100–$125
Pat and Mike	1952	MGM	$40–$50
Pawnshop, The (Charlie Chaplin)	1916	Mutual	$500–$600
Singin' in the Rain	1952	MGM	$60–$75
Jumbo lobby card (14" x 17", horizontal or vertical)			
Her Wedding Night (Clara Bow)	1930	Paramount	$200–$250
State Fair (Janet Gaynor)	1933	Fox	$125–$150
Window card (14" x 22", vertical)			
Bullitt (Steve McQueen)	1968	Warner Bros.	$150–$180
Clash by Night	1952	RKO	$125–$150
Gold Diggers of 1933	1933	Warner Bros.	$800–$1,000
Moon over Miami (Betty Grable)	1941	Twentieth Century Fox	$400–$500
2001: A Space Odyssey	1968	MGM	$200–$250
Jumbo window card (22" x 28", vertical)			
Belle Starr	1941	Twentieth Century Fox	$350–$400
Conqueror, The (John Wayne/Susan Hayward)	1956	RKO	$40–$50

Film	Year	Studio	Value
Insert (14" x 36", vertical)			
Body and Soul	1947	United Artists	$500–$600
Bus Stop (Marilyn Monroe)	1956	Twentieth Century Fox	$500–$600
Logan's Run	1976	MGM	$40–$50
Patsy, The	1964	Paramount	$25–$30
Rocky	1976	United Artists	$120–$125
Display or half-sheet (22" x 28", horizontal)			
Chinatown (Jack Nicholson)	1974	Paramount	$200–$250
Jason and the Argonauts	1963	Columbia	$100–$125
Karate Kid, The	1984	Columbia	$30–$35
Lord of the Rings, The	1978	United Artists	$40–$50
Pretty Baby	1978	Paramount	$30–$35
One-sheet (27" x 41", vertical)			
Cabaret	1972	Allied Artists	$200–$250
Casino (Robert De Niro/Sharon Stone)	1995	Universal	$65–$85
Hangover Square	1945	Twentieth Century Fox	$400–$500
Independence Day	1996	Twentieth Century Fox	$20–$25
Jaws	1975	Universal	$300–$375
Jurassic Park	1993	Universal	$30–$35
Risky Business	1983	Warner Bros.	$40–$50
Rocky Horror Picture Show, The (Style A, "Lips")	1975	Twentieth Century Fox	$100–$125
Susan and God (Joan Crawford)	1940	MGM	$400–$500
Three-sheet (two or three horizontal sheets assembling to 41" x 81", vertical)			
Cool Hand Luke (Paul Newman)	1967	Warner Bros.	$650–$800
Little Shop of Horrors, The	1960	Filmgroup	$200–$250
Mary Poppins	1964	Disney/Buena Vista	$350–$450
30" x 40" (vertical)			
Never Say Never Again	1983	Warner Bros.	$150–$175
Rescuers, The	1977	Disney/Buena Vista	$50–$60
Rooster Cogburn (John Wayne/Katharine Hepburn)	1975	Universal	$100–$125
40" x 60" (vertical)			
Barbarella	1968	Paramount	$300–$350
Creepshow	1982	Warner Bros.	$100–$125
Mad Max (Mel Gibson)	1979	Warner Bros.	$200–$250
Meteor	1979	American International	$40–$50
Six-sheet (four sheets assembling to 81" x 81")			
Close Encounters of the Third Kind	1977	Columbia	$200–$250
Let It Be (Beatles)	1970	United Artists	$400–$500
Sand Pebbles, The (Steve McQueen)	1966	Twentieth Century Fox	$250–$300
Twenty-four-sheet (9' x 20', horizontal)			
Goldfinger	1964	United Artists	$1,200–$1,500
King of Kings, The	1927	Pathé	$3,000–$4,000

GLOSSARY

big paper   Three-, six-, and twenty-four-sheet posters.

Motion Picture Production Code of 1930 (Hays Code)   One of the most far-reaching moralistic guidelines ever imposed on an American industry by public sentiment and threat of government action (read the full text at http://www.artsreformation.com/a001/hays-code.html). A watershed in American filmmaking, reflecting a strong conservative reaction to the adventuresome, sometimes morally risqué content of films produced up to that time. It remained in force until the 1960s.

photogelatin process   This printing method utilized a metal plate covered with a photosensitized gelatin, which was exposed to light through a photographic negative. Popular from the 1920s through the 1950s, it yielded an exceptionally clear image. This process was used for half-sheets, inserts, and lobby cards, since they were designed to be viewed at close range.

photo lithography   A printing process using photographically prepared plates that came into use for posters around 1935, supplanting the hand-drawn poster and satisfying the desire of movie fans and theater owners for accuracy in reproducing the likenesses of their favorite stars. Images were translated by offset lithography into a pattern of dots; the thicker the concentration of dots, the heavier the tone.

stone lithography   The process of printing from a flat surface on which an image is drawn and/or painted by hand with an oily crayon or other greasy substance on a porous stone or, later, a metal plate. The design is then fixed, the entire surface is moistened, and printing ink is applied, adhering only to the oily lines or areas. This process, which yields exceptionally rich tones and colors, was used for making movie posters from the earliest days until (by a few studios) the 1940s.

BIBLIOGRAPHY AND
RECOMMENDED READING

Bridges, Herb. *"Frankly, My Dear ...": Gone with the Wind Memorabilia*. Macon, Ga.: Mercer University Press, 1995.

Citadel Press. *The Films of . . . Errol Flynn, Joan Crawford, Bing Crosby*, etc. New York and Secaucus, N.J.

    Comments: A series of individual volumes published in the 1960s and 1970s on all the major stars. They're great for identifying stills. Although long out of print, they can be found at secondhand bookstores.

Finler, Joel W. *Hollywood Movie Stills. The Golden Age*. London: B. T. Batsford, 1995.

Fricke, John. *100 Years of Oz*. New York: Stewart, Tabori & Chang, 1999.

Fricke, John, Jay Scarfone, and William Stillman. *The Wizard of Oz: The Official 50th Anniversary Pictorial History*. New York: Warner Books, 1989.

Hake, Ted. *Hake's Guide to Cowboy Character Collectibles*. Radnor, Pa.: Wallace-Homestead, 1994.

———. *Hake's Price Guide to Character Toys*. 2d ed. New York: Avon Books, 1998.

Hardy, Phil, ed. *The Western*. The Overlook Film Encyclopedia Series. Woodstock, N.Y.: Overlook Press, 1994.

    Comments: Contains entries on important A and B Westerns from the 1930s to the 1980s, plus a complete listing of all Westerns from the sound period. Other encyclopedias from the series cover science fiction, horror, and film noir.

Heide, Robert, and John Gilman. *Starstruck: The Wonderful World of Movie Memorabilia*. New York: Doubleday, 1986.

Huxford, Bob, and Sharon Huxford. *Huxford's Old Book Value Guide*. 12th ed. Paducah, Ky.: Collector Books, 2000.

Kisch, John, ed. *Poster Price Almanac*. Hyde Park, N.Y.: Separate Cinema Publications, 2001.

Kobal, John, ed. *50 Years of Movie Posters*. New York: Crown Publishers, 1973.

Cape Fear, 1962, Universal, three-sheet. Film noir classics such as *Cape Fear* attract substantial collector interest. *Photo courtesy of Chisholm-Larsson Gallery.*

Loehr, David, and Joe Bills. *The James Dean Collectors Guide.* Gas City, Ind.: L-W Book Sales, 1999.

Maltin, Leonard, et al. *Leonard Maltin's 2001 Movie & Video Guide.* New York: Signet, 2001.

Mills, Brian. *A Collector's Guide to Movie Star Memorabilia.* London: B. T. Batsford, 1991.

Pardella, Edward R. *Shirley Temple Dolls and Fashions.* West Chester, Pa.: Schiffer Publishing, 1992.

———. *The Judy Garland Collector's Guide.* West Chester, Pa.: Schiffer Publishing, 1999.

Proddow, Penny, et al. *Hollywood Jewels: Movies, Jewelry, Stars.* New York: Harry N. Abrams, 1996.

Scarfone, Jay, and William Stillman. *The Wizard of Oz, Collector's Treasury.* West Chester, Pa.: Schiffer Publishing, 1992.

———. *The Wizardry of Oz.* New York: Gramercy, 1999.

Schapiro, Steve, and David Chierichetti. The Movie Poster Book. New York: E. P. Dutton, 1979.

Semling, Brian. *Beckett's Everything You Need to Know about Collecting Star Wars Collectibles.* Dallas, Tex.: Beckett, 1998.

Stephan, Elizabeth, ed. *O'Brien's Collecting Toys: Identification and Value Guide.* 9th ed. Iola, Wis.: Krause, 1999.

ABOUT THE INTERNATIONAL SOCIETY OF APPRAISERS

The Collector's Compass series is endorsed by the International Society of Appraisers, one of North America's leading nonprofit associations of professionally educated and certified personal-property appraisers. Members of the ISA include many of the industry's most respected independent appraisers, auctioneers, and dealers. ISA appraisers specialize in more than two hundred areas of expertise in four main specialty pathways: antiques and residential contents, fine art, gems and jewelry, and machinery and equipment.

Established in 1979 and consisting of more than 1,375 members, the ISA is founded on two core principles: educating its members through a wide range of continuing education and training opportunities, and promoting and maintaining the highest ethical and professional standards in the field of appraisals.

Education through the ISA

In conjunction with the University of Maryland University College, the ISA offers a series of post-secondary professional courses in appraisal studies, including a two-level certification program.

The ISA recognizes three membership levels within its organization—Associate Member, Accredited Member, and Certified Member—with educational programs in place for achieving higher distinctions within the society. ISA members who complete the required coursework are recognized with the title of Certified Appraiser of Personal Property (CAPP). Through its pioneering education programs, the ISA plays a vital role in producing qualified appraisers in appraisal theory, principles, procedures, ethics, and law as it pertains to personal-property appraisal.

Professional Standards of the ISA

The ISA is dedicated to the highest ethical standards of conduct, ensuring public confidence in the ability and qualifications of its members. To help members perform their work with the most up-to-date knowledge of professional standards, the ISA is continually updating, expanding, and improving its courses and criteria of conduct.

For more information about the International Society of Appraisers, contact its corporate offices:

Toll-free: 800-472-4732
E-mail: ISAHQ@isa-appraisers.org
Web site: www.isa-appraisers.org

ABOUT THE CONTRIBUTORS

Todd R. Feiertag's passion for movie posters was sparked on Saturday afternoons during the 1950s, at Brooklyn's Graham Theater. In 1963, his family moved to suburban Orangeburg, New York. One day, young Todd simply asked a local theater manager if a poster or two might be given away. Thanks to that manager's response, a world-class collection got its start.

By the mid-1970s, following college, Mr. Feiertag began collecting in earnest—buying from the handful of movie-poster dealers then in business. By the end of the decade, his collecting had evolved into his own company—Poster City—which by 1982 was operating a gallery in Nyack, New York, as well as producing mail-order movie-poster catalogs with thousands of items for sale. On March 1, 1997, Sotheby's New York conducted an auction of nearly four hundred poster lots from Mr. Feiertag's collection, which produced the highest price paid to date for a single poster—$453,500 for a one-sheet from the 1932 film *The Mummy*—more than double the previous record.

In addition to his collecting and selling, Todd Feiertag has been a contributor to books on movie posters, including *Reel Art: Great Posters from the Age of the Silver Screen* by Stephen Rebello and Richard Allen (Abbeville, 1988) and *Starstruck: The Wonderful World of Movie Memorabilia* by Robert Heide and John Gilman (Doubleday, 1986). He has also appeared on CNBC, CNN, and FX as an expert on movie posters as investments.

Mr. Feiertag continues to operate Poster City at P.O. Box 94, Orangeburg, NY 10962, 800-272-3323, e-mail toddfeiertag@msn.com.

Judith Katz-Schwartz began running a part-time antiques-and-collectibles business while working as a chef and corporate food executive. In 1986 she founded Twin Brooks Antiques and Collectibles, and the next year she opened an independent appraisal practice. Since 1993, she has been doing business online at www.msjudith.net.

Ms. Katz-Schwartz has been featured as a collectibles expert on numerous television and radio shows, among them Fox Entertainment's top-rated FX cable network show *Personal FX* and Pax TV's *Treasures in Your Home*. She writes, edits, and publishes *The Antiques and Collectibles Newsletter*, an offbeat e-mail newsletter about collecting, and is moderator of the Collectibles & Memorabilia Forum on the *AntiqueWeek* Web site. She lives in Manhattan and Sullivan County, New York, with her husband, Arthur Schwartz.

Michael B. King has been hooked on movies since 1940, when he saw *Pinocchio,* his first film experience. By age fourteen, he was buying stills and posters to advertise the silent films he exhibited in his basement theater to the accompaniment of Paul Whiteman records on a windup Victrola. In the early 1960s, as head of the art department at Brooks School in North Andover, Massachusetts, he was teaching studio art, art history, photography, and film. It was at this point that he began collecting movie memorabilia in earnest to use as artifacts in his courses in film, which he co-taught with E. Graham Ward. In 1973 he appeared as guest columnist in Leonard Maltin's *Film Fan Monthly,* and then contributing editor until it ceased publication in 1975. Mr. King is currently director of the Robert Lehman Art Center at Brooks School. He lives in Dublin, New Hampshire, and can be reached at mbking@mcttelecom.com.

Christopher J. Kuppig has spent his entire career in book publishing. For several years he directed programs at Dell Publishing, Consumer Reports Books, and most recently Chilton Book Company—where his assignments included managing the Wallace-Homestead and Warman's lines of antiques-and-collectibles guides.

In 1997, Mr. Kuppig founded Stone Studio Publishing Services, a general management consultancy to book publishers. Acting as series editor for the Collector's Compass series has given him the opportunity to draw upon his wide-ranging network of contacts in the collecting field.

Mr. Kuppig resides with his wife and three children in eastern Massachusetts.

INDEX

Note: Page numbers in italics denote information in a photo or caption.

A

action figures. *See* figurals *and* toys
appraisals, 83, 118, 124
artists, 8, 10, *54,* 70, 74
auctions, live, 10, 24, 32, 38–39, 41–43, 110, 116
  See also Internet auctions
authenticity, 36–39, 72–73, 76, 100
autographs, 7, 72–73

B

bally books. *See* press books
Bergman, Ingrid, *56, 91*
Bogart, Humphrey, *28–29, 56, 58*
Bond, James, *12,* 12–13, *104*
books, 23
Bow, Clara, 46, *47,* 99, 119
Bull, Clarence Sinclair, 97, *98,* 101

C

calendars, 17, 80
campaign manuals. *See* press books
cards
  scene, *58, 61*
  lobby. *See* lobby cards
  playing, 12
  trading, 13, 81
  window. *See* window cards
Casablanca, 10, *56*
Chaplin, Charlie, *18–19, 19,* 47, 72, *108,* 119
Christie's, 13, 24, 29, 38–39, *52,* 113
Citizen Kane, 58, 80

Columbia, *15, 49, 54,* 86, 119, 120
commissions, 37, 41, 42, 107, 110
condition, 36, 43, 48, 66–68, 99
costumes, 8, 38
Crawford, Joan, 46, 98, 99, 101, *101,* 119

D

damage, 43, 66–68, 99
dating, 71–72
Davis, Bette, *16,* 58
dealers, 30–32, 42, 82–83, 115–116
  Internet, 24, 68, 73
  and pricing, 9, 14, 34–36
  selling to, 106–107
Dean, James, 8, 17, 81
Dietrich, Marlene, *55, 57*
Disney, 38, *52,* 85–86, 120
displays, 21
dolls, 26–27, 92, 112–113
  See also figurals *and* toys

E

ephemera, 80–81
exchanges, 20
  See also National Screen Service

F

figurals, 7, 8, 13, 92
  value of, 26–27
  See also dolls *and* toys
flea markets, 9, 17, 31
Flynn, Errol, *64,* 101, *102*
formats. *See* movie-paper formats
frames, 38–39
framing, 94–96
Frankenstein, 14, 31, 69, 76

G

Gable, Clark, *49,* 84, *84,* 92
games, 13, 26, 92
Garbo, Greta, 24, 46, 97–98, *98,* 99
Garland, Judy, 26, *61, 112,* 112–113
glass slides, 19, 46–48, *57*
Gone with the Wind, 92–93, *93*

H

Hitchcock, Alfred, *59, 91,* 109

I

inserts, 21, *36,* 120
insurance, 82–83
Internet auctions, 13, 23, 37–41, 100, 113, 117–118
  bargains on, 14, 31
  locating memorabilia, 10, 17, 24, 27, 44, 47, 81, 87, 93
  selling on, 107–110
  See also auctions, live
inventory, 82–83, 105–106

K

Karloff, Boris, 14, *51, 69, 103*
King Kong, 33, *63,* 70, 76, 86, 97
kitsch, 7–8, 17

L

lithography, *19,* 21–22, *53*
  See also printing processes
lobby cards, 7, 20, 21, *22, 40, 42, 49, 57–59, 61, 62, 111*
  bargains, 31, 33

condition, 66
framing, 69, 95
value, 119

M

magazines. *See* publications
Marx Brothers, *62,* 72, 80
Metropolis, 22, 24, 47, *57,*
99
MGM, 11, *40, 55, 60, 61,*
74, 78, 109, 111,
112–113, 119
press books, 84, 86
still photos, 97–98, *98,*
99–101, *101,* 102, 103
Monroe, Marilyn, 72, 75,
75, 80–81, 96, 120
novelty items, 17, 80–81
still photos, 97, 99
movie-paper formats, 20,
21, 22, 90
Mummy, The, 14, 22,
50–51, 70, 72–73, 76

N

National Screen Service,
20–21, 97

O

offset printing. *See* printing
processes
online auctions. *See*
Internet auctions

P

Paramount, 11, *43,* 46, *47,*
50, 55, 59, 62, 88,
119, 120
still photos, 99, 102
plates, 7, 8, 92, 113
posters, 29–32, *50–55,*
59–60, 62–64, 91
condition, 66–69
framing, 89–95
history of, 7–9, 19–21,
71–72
packaging, 65–66, 84
rarity, 72–73
repairs, 95
reproductions, 76–78

value of, 11, 14–15,
24–25, 82, 120
preservation, 67, 70,
89–90, 94–96, 103
press books, 7, 73–74,
84–87
press kits, 7, 84–87
printing processes, 21–22,
73
programs, *80,* 80
props, 8, 38–39
publications, 10, 12, 45,
80, 116–117
locating memorabilia, 10,
30, 32, 41
and selling, 108,
110–111
See also books

R

rarities, 66, 72, 79, 82
receipts, 36, 44, 72, 82–83
record keeping, 30, 36, 82,
105–106
reissues, 77–78
repairs, 68–70, 95, 103
reproductions, 21–22, 29,
31, 76
reserve prices, 40, 42–43
returns, 36, 37, 40–41
RKO, *52, 58, 61, 63, 80,*
86, *91,* 119
still photos, 102

S

scenery, 38–39
scripts, 38, *39*
selling memorabilia,
105–111
shops, specialty, 30
shows, 10, 24, 27, 32, 47,
81, 87, 100, 114
Sotheby's, 14, 24, 29,
38–39, 86
Spielberg, Steven, *6–7, 79*
Star Wars, 7, 8, 9, 10, 15,
15, 23, 38, 44–45, *45*
still photos, 7, *33, 79, 81,*
109

history of, 19–20, 87,
97–103
stone lithography. *See*
lithography
storage, 90

T

Temple, Shirley, 15, 27,
119
toys, 26–27, 112–113
Twentieth Century Fox,
15, 16, 25, 45, 71, *96,*
119, 120
2001: A Space Odyssey, 78,
103, 119

U

UFA/Paramount, *22, 57*
United Artists, *12, 39, 52,*
86, 95, *104,* 120
Universal, *7,* 11, 46,
50–51, 86, 120, *123*
still photos, *79,* 99,
101–102, *103*

V

value, 44, 47, 80–81, 106,
112–113
figurals, 26–27
fluctuations in, 11
lobby cards, 33, 119
posters, 66–76, 120
press books, 86
still photos, 99

W

Warner Bros., 11, *28, 29,*
33, 56, 58, 59, 62, 64,
71, 113, 119, 120
still photos, 101, *102*
Web sites, 23, 37–39, 73,
114–118
locating memorabilia, 13,
31, 81, 93
Westerns, 10, 27, *53,* 85
window cards, 21, 66–67,
69, *88,* 119
Wizard of Oz, The, 8, 10,
61, 86, *112,* 112–113